THE

USER FRIENDLY GUIDE™

ble!

THE WEB GURU GUIDE

The Entrepreneur's Internet Marketing Bible!

By Josh B. Dolin

Published by BG Publishing International

The Web Guru Guide

Published by BG Publishing International
1304 SW 160th Avenue, #203, Sunrise FL 33326

Visit us on the web at www.BGPublishingInternational.com

ISBN -13: 978-0-9624333-8-2

To Asher,
An exciting life lies ahead.

TABLE OF CONTENTS

Foreword by Sheila Danzig

I have enjoyed being an author, speaker, consultant, and reporter for more than four decades. As a result, I have witnessed firsthand the amazing potential for advertising and publicity exposure that has resulted from the Internet's increased accessibility and popularity. Many of my clients have reaped sizable financial benefits and experienced substantial growth in revenues as a result of online advertising and web marketing techniques developed over the last decade.

I was delighted when Josh asked me to collaborate with him on his new book about website design and marketing. I was even more flattered when he asked me to write the foreword. During my career in Internet sales and eMarketing, I have received many titles, such as "Internet Guru" and "Queen of the Net." Once, I was even named one of the "44 Most Famous Internet Marketers."

One of the reasons I have received these recognitions is because I have been working in the publicity business since long before the Internet existed. I developed a computer-based marketing approach during the early years of the computer age, in the decades when cassette players were standard options in automobiles. As the Internet has evolved, so too have my electronic advertising techniques and marketing approaches. Acknowledging the power of the Internet, and using it to maximize business exposure and profit share, is critical to corporate success. Technology continues to grow rapidly with each passing year. Our world depends greatly on telecommunications and electronic technology. Indeed, the computer is capable of producing almost everything except the physical essentials of life – food, water, and sunlight!

As our digital dependence continues to grow, the opportunities for professional Internet marketing increase as well. Because many web design experts are afraid to share their secrets and offer advice for fear of losing a prospective client, many smaller business owners are missing out on these opportunities. Fortunately, Josh isn't like this. Instead of viewing his wide range of expertise as proprietary intellectual property, he is willing to share his insights with small business owners to help them grow their businesses. Josh does this by delivering key concepts and ideas to readers in an informative, casual style that makes practical application almost unbelievably easy.

Small business owners will find this concise, understandable information a precious gift that will help them develop new growth and marketing strategies. Take advantage of this opportunity to implement these strategies now, while other businesses are still struggling to recover from a severe recession. Josh uses this book to introduce and explain proven web marketing methods that can and do work. Furthermore, he does so using a relaxed, easy teaching format that even a PC novice can quickly grasp and utilize.

As in past decades, corporate processes continue to evolve and change. To maintain pace with these changing times, company managers and business owners must adjust and evolve as well. For many people over forty, this means leaving our comfort zones and jumping into the digital age. Unfortunately, the "word of mouth" techniques popularly used by businesses during past decades are no longer as effective as many business professionals still prefer to think.

I am fully confident that entrepreneurs throughout the international business arena will review and explore the marketing techniques Josh discusses. In his book, he proves the axiom I have long advocated to my clients: Effective marketing does not seem or appear to be marketing. In fact, when you employ the simple but very powerful concepts he shares, you may not even consciously realize that you are using marketing skills. That is because these skills are imperative, effective, yet unobtrusive.

I truly hope you enjoy this book as much as I have enjoyed being a part of it. This is definitely a book you will read and re-read in order to glean every possible gem of marketing wisdom that can help your business experience enormous growth potential through the power of the Internet.

Introduction by Josh Dolin

The Internet is the most popular source of information and advertising in our 21st century world today. Although it initially began as a small, proprietary service for electronic mail and news sharing, it has rapidly advanced in terms of content and resource utilization. Today, people access the resources available through the Internet to seek medical advice, conduct educational research, read the news, and skim the latest celebrity gossip. They shop at online auction sites, buy clothing through Internet retailers, and even purchase home theater systems or appliances from eCommerce stores.

The rapid advance in the popularity of the Internet can be demonstrated effectively in a single statistic. In 2001, 45 percent of the American public had at least one email address. Today, 80 percent of the people in the United States have an email address. Internet communication is the single most rapidly advancing technology today. As a result, website marketing is an essential advertising foundation for all small businesses, including both online and local, brick-and-mortar companies.

Many business owners regularly email business contacts as well as friends and family. They may even order supplies online, scan the business news, or monitor the Dow. Some, however, neglect to explore the enormous business growth potential made available by the Internet. They are unaware that the Internet is the single avenue by which a business can reach the entire world.

My goal in writing The Web Guru Guide© was to create a tool that offered small business owners the opportunity to begin utilizing the infinite capabilities offered by the Internet. If you are among the many professionals who find the concepts of successful web marketing overwhelming and intimidating, stop worrying. Any business owner can incorporate these advertising and marketing strategies and enjoy the profits and growth that result. eMarketing techniques, contrary to what you and other professionals might imagine, are not too difficult to use. If you follow the simple, but effective, methods I share in these chapters, you too can increase revenues and achieve a far greater sales potential than you previously imagined possible.

I am the owner and founder of a successful web design and marketing company called Tempo Creative. My corporate team creates successful web marketing strategies for businesses and corporations that require a complete range of Internet marketing services to successfully sell and promote their products or services. My clients are small business owners and large corporations. Tempo Creative provides a comprehensive package of services based on each individual company's unique needs and characteristics.

I believe, though, that an entrepreneur or small business owner can do much to promote a small, successful local business using basic, straightforward methods. These are the same tools and techniques we use at Tempo Creative to make our firm, and ultimately our clients, highly successful. My purpose in writing this book is to share some of these methods and teach you how to implement them yourself. Using them, you can develop a profitable strategy that works well for your business.

This book isn't filled with technical information about learning HTML, PHP or any of the other complex languages used in coding and web design. Nor will this book be used to teach professional graphic design-like courses offered at the local community college or university. My goal isn't to convince you to embark on a new career as a website design consultant. Instead, I want to lay a foundation and teach you the fundamentals of eMarketing.

Let me encourage you, the small business owner, to take your company's eMarketing into your own hands and realize a higher growth potential than you ever thought imaginable. I challenge you to take the helpful information contained in this book and use it to help your business recognize its potential. Or, if you lack the time or employee resources to implement these strategies yourself, contact me directly for assistance, or arrange a consultation by visiting me at TheWebGuruGuide. com.

Thank you for taking valuable time to read this book. I hope you enjoy it. Finally, I know that if you take the time to employ the techniques and tools I share, your business will benefit. I wish you great success and happiness in your business ventures!

Chapter One: Creativity is Key

"Creativity is the power to connect the seemingly unconnected."

– William Plomer

The keys to a successful marketing strategy, like any other quality project, include careful planning, creativity, and innovation. If you're already a successful business owner, you may be tempted to skip the first few paragraphs, sure that you already understand the fundamental concepts of launching and marketing a business. Avoid this temptation, though, so that you don't miss an important element that might help you to be even more successful. I want you to achieve optimal outcomes, so let's start by reviewing the basics. By doing this, we can approach essential marketing techniques from the same perspective.

If you haven't already launched your business, and are trying to get a solid grasp on the basics before starting, read and re-read this information until you've internalized all of these ideas. Develop a solid foundation for understanding marketing techniques, and then put these ideas into practice. I guarantee you that the time you invest won't be wasted!

The first step in operating a successful business venture is to identify the target of the products or services being marketed. The target is the person or group that will be buying the product or using the service offered by the company. After identifying the target, you, the business owner, face the difficult task of developing a marketing strategy that will reach the target and persuade that person or group that your business offers the exact product or service necessary.

Accomplishing this requires creativity and expertise. These qualities help a service provider or business organization to develop a marketing approach that causes the company to compete successfully against other companies offering similar merchandise or services. Many corporations offer quality products, and some of these products may be similar or even identical to yours. Marketing strategies that make logical connections between related concepts and products are relatively easy to develop, but they lack a "hook," or angle, that will give the user an edge over the competition. The key to gaining this edge is to find a marketing approach that presents information creatively. Doing this requires the expertise of a true guru.

As I explained in the introduction to this book, most people search online for a wide variety of products and services. Almost everyone under age 40 is more likely to search online for a business, service, or website, than to open the Yellow Pages of their local telephone book. Websites help us to compare prices, make travel plans, rate physicians, and use review guides to avoid inferior service providers. Therefore, the first secret to successful eMarketing is to develop a creative, informative website that attracts viewers.

Today, the majority of business owners, service providers, non-profit organizations, and educational institutions have recognized that a web presence is vital to their existence. Most have, at the very least, developed a website that lists essential information such as contact details, a list of products or services, a logo, and a picture or two. In 1995, when my Internet career began, this was more than enough. Today, however, web technology and speedy Internet connections permit – and encourage – much higher standards for website design and creativity than were possible in the early 1990s.

Consider this example: Two business owners decide to launch Internet merchant (e-commerce) sites that sell downloadable software, or shareware. One decides to design a website utilizing minimal graphics that does not employ creative marketing strategies. The other owner hires a creative consultant to develop a marketing approach for the company with a carefully conceptualized website design. Both companies choose to market identical products.

You can already guess which company is more likely to be successful. The owner who invested in a professional website is much more likely to draw visitors, or traffic. He or she is also much more likely to generate a higher rate of service, or product revenue. Developing a creative, informative company website is the most effective way to deliver business-related information to a broad spectrum of visitors.

Now, let's discuss how to use creativity to develop an eMarketing concept for your business that demonstrates you to be a "guru" in your field. The following sections will help you to identify and secure a catchy, appropriate domain name.

Catchy Domain Names

Before beginning to discuss design strategies, you will need to secure a domain name that hasn't already been registered. Keep in mind that the ideal domain name for your business is one that incorporates your company's name. Some business owners elect to use domain names that contain an acronym of the business's name. This is usually most effective, though, for large, well-recognized companies like banks and utilities. For example, the corporate website for the National Football League is NFL.com. Similarly, PGE.com houses the website presence for Pacific Gas and Electric Company. Unless your business is nationally recognized, though, it is generally best to avoid using an acronym of your company's name when registering a domain name.

To see how this could be problematic, consider the possible consequences of abbreviating a business name such as Peggy's Grill Emporium or New Frames, Limited. First, most domain names using these acronyms are likely to be already registered to the larger corporations represented by these same acronyms. Additionally, while people may find your website accidentally, during their search for information about professional football or utility companies, many will not find this to be a fortunate accident. Finally, prospective visitors may search for your company, locate the utility or sport website, and decide that they have the wrong name. These visitors will never reach your website.

Generally, a good website for a business is one that includes the company's name. Consider a company that is incorporated as Stevenson Accounting Services. A good website for a business like this might be www.

stevensonaccounting.com. Remember, however, that while you can use as many as 67 characters for a domain name, longer names are more likely to be forgotten or mistyped than shorter names. Choosing long, complicated names may cause you to lose business. Keep the name short, catchy, and representative of your business.

Product Specific Names

Whenever possible, choose a name that reflects your service or product. For example, most religious institutions use their organization's name in their domain names. Since many organizations have the same name, some also use the city or state in which they are located.

Similarly, cultural organizations, healthcare organizations, and even e-commerce sites use domain names that reflect their purpose. For instance, the Metropolitan Museum of Art uses the domain name MetMuseum.org, and Stanford University can be reached by typing Stanford. edu.

Choose a name that best reflects your company's service or product. Then, visitors and clients will easily associate the domain name with the business name. This, in turn, will increase the likelihood that they visit – and return to – your website.

Keep it Simple

Again, keep the domain name relevant, but avoid long names that are difficult to remember. Even though a domain name can include up to 67 characters, most people are unlikely to remember character strings this long. If possible, try to use a domain name that is 20 characters or less in length. At the same time, however, try to avoid using acronyms that no one knows or understands. Focus on names that people will find, remember and spell easily.

Some professionals choose to use hyphens in the domain name to represent their business. Hyphenated names are sometimes helpful because they usually are still available for purchase and registry even when the unhyphenated domain name is already being used. In addition, these names often receive better rankings with search engines, because the words are separated and easy to distinguish.

Hyphenated names also have some disadvantages that can limit their use, however. First, hyphens are harder to remember and inconvenient to type. As a result, visitors may locate a competitor's site more easily than yours. Additionally, when talking about your site, clients, friends, or family members may forget to mention the hyphens, so these potential referrals may not be able to locate your website.

Domain Name Extensions: .com, .org, .net and many more!

Many people make the mistake of purchasing and registering domain names without considering the significant differences between .com, .org, and .net extensions. eMarketing novices often don't realize that the differences between domain extensions can make the critical difference between the success – and failure – of their marketing endeavors. They choose a name believing that .com sites will always guarantee the greatest exposure, but this isn't always the case.

For instance, if you are planning a website that will host a non-profit organization, be aware that most religious institutions, charity groups, and other agencies use domains names with .org extensions. For example, the American Red Cross has registered the domain name RedCross.org. As a general rule, unless you're creating a website for a non-profit organization, avoid choosing a .org extension. If your goal, however, is to design a site for one of these types of organizations, you will probably want to consider a domain name that includes this extension.

Sometimes, finding a good .com name for a business can be difficult, because these are very popular and quickly chosen. Because of this, some people opt instead to choose domain names with .net extensions. This can result in poorer search engine rankings because the algorithms used by search engines typically rank .com results first. As a result, a business competitor with a similar domain name and a .com extension may have a better chance than a .net business of drawing site visitors. If you do choose to use .net for your business website, be sure to emphasize that extension when advertising or promoting the site.

Some businesses choose to avoid this problem by registering both .com and .net domains for their websites. Corporations do this in an attempt to minimize traffic loss to competitors. AT&T is one example of a corporation that does this. Searchers who type ATT.net or ATT.com will be directed to AT&T's homepage. If you intend to do this, search and confirm that both .com and .net extensions containing your domain name are available when you register. Then, register the names simultaneously so that a competitor does not register using the alternate extension.

One other possible pitfall in choosing a domain name can trap unwary business owners. Many people who are unfamiliar with the process of choosing a domain name are unaware that country-specific locations, such as .us or .uk, can limit traffic. If your business sells a product or service that is specific to a certain country or region, consider using a country specific location. As an example, insurance companies who are providing policies only to drivers in the United Kingdom may find it helpful to register a domain name with a .uk extension.

If you aren't planning to limit your business to a specific region or country, however, you will probably want to avoid using country-specific locations. Avoid the temptation to do this just to register a preferred domain name. These extensions often don't help, and can even sometimes hurt, traffic generation.

There are a plethora of additional domain name extensions available, such as .co, .info, .me, and .biz to name a few. While it's not necessary to register every domain extension for your business, it makes sense to own the most important ones to avoid conflicts with your competition. I'd recommend registering .com and .net without hesitation, and choosing several others based on your type of business.

Registering a Domain Name

After deciding on a domain name, the next step is to register the domain. I have found that GoDaddy.com offers the easiest and most cost-effective approach for registering and managing a domain. Once you have selected the name, register at GoDaddy or a similar site. Check to ensure that the chosen domain name or names are still available, and then register them. In some cases, the name may already be registered by another individual or business entity. Then, you will have to decide whether to select a different name or, if the desired name is for sale, pay the price the registered user is asking.

Domain Names: 21st Century Real Estate

I mentioned earlier that a desired domain name might already be registered. But, sometimes a user will decide to register the name and then sell the registry to another person or company. This type of transaction has become so popular that some enterprising entrepreneurs view domain name registry as the 21st century version of real estate investment. Domain name brokers have made millions of dollars registering and reselling domain names to business owners willing to pay top prices for their choice of domain names. You may not be interested in domain name speculation as a business investment, but consider possible future business ventures when choosing a name. Registering these domain names may cost you as little as $7 annually. This small investment, however, may save you the thousands of dollars it could cost to purchase that name from a domain broker in a few years. Finally, that $7 domain you purchased in 2010 might be worth $7,000 or more in 2020!

Summing it up:

Important points to remember about domain names:

• Whenever possible, use a domain name that is identical or similar to the business name.

• Avoid acronyms, unless your business or organization is very large or well-known.

• Hyphens and plurals are often hard to remember, and may lead potential customers straight to your competitors.

• Try to keep the domain name to 20 characters or less when possible.

• Remember that .com websites are always indexed first, but there are other domain extensions that are worthy of consideration.

Chapter Two: Appealing Graphics

"Design is a plan for arranging elements in such a way as best to accomplish a particular purpose."

– Charles Eames

Most business professionals reading this book will easily grasp the importance of relevant website content, or copy. Visitors seek specific information when they visit a website. The type of information available depends on the site's purpose. For example, clients browsing a dentist's website may want to learn more about office policies and dental procedures. They will also want to find contact information and office hours. In comparison, visitors to a technology consultant's website will want to learn what services are available and how a consultation can be arranged.

What many people don't realize, however, is that graphics are almost as important as good writing. Graphics help to break up blocks of text. They also create a visually stimulating and entertaining page that encourages visitors to return. Creative graphics help to emphasize important information, draw the reader's eye to key points, and create memorable mental images of the page. Website design experts understand that eye-catching graphics make the critical difference between a boring website filled with columns of copy and an appealing, interactive page that draws visitors in – and keeps them returning for more.

Choosing and Using Graphics

Now that you understand the importance of graphics, you're probably wondering what kind of graphics you should use. Generally, the graphics used on your business's website should reflect the products, services, or mission of your company or organization. Some people prefer to commission graphic designers to create a custom image or logo for their website. Others prefer to use candid or professional photos depicting the corporation's employees. Whichever you choose, be sure to choose graphics that reflect the image you wish your corporation to project. Don't make the mistake of choosing images or photos that could become a source of personal or professional embarrassment to you or your employees.

Graphics also offer an excellent avenue for emphasizing new content or directing visitors to special sale prices. Visitors usually don't return to a website hoping to find the same content with no new graphics or images each time they visit. In fact, if websites fail to provide updated content or new photos, repeat traffic drops off quickly, and search engine rankings will fall rapidly as well. To prevent this, choose creative graphics, use them wisely, and change or update them as needed.

Understand though, that maintaining some degree of consistency is also important. Choose a logo that complements the business's corporate image, and use that logo regularly throughout the website. Furthermore, use background and text colors that coordinate with, and do not clash with, the graphics and logo. We'll discuss colors in detail later in the book, but for now, follow this general rule: If you wouldn't be seen wearing a particular shirt and tie color combination, avoid trying to coordinate those colors on your corporate website.

One excellent way to personalize graphics is to post

pictures portraying the office staff on the "About Us" page. This will help to personalize the business and make it more appealing to visitors. Use this page to draw visitors in and encourage them to feel a connection with the company. This will make them want to keep returning to the website as well.

While professional photos can help a staff to look its best, these are usually fairly expensive. Furthermore, they aren't always necessary. Often, good candid shots with a digital camera can accomplish the same effect. Again, however, remember to display pictures that are in good taste. Include only images that reflect the company's ethical and social standards. For instance, you may be tempted to share photos from the office Christmas party with your clients or friends. Images of relaxed, friendly staff members are appealing; photos of professional people overindulging or wearing inappropriate attire are not!

Another effective technique is to utilize pictures that reflect the service or product marketed by the company. For example, a web design company might include photos of its staff designing a graphic or logo, editing copy, or conferring about a design layout in front of a computer. Similarly, a dog grooming business may choose to post photos of its clients posing proudly after a bathing and brushing. Always remember, however, to have employees, clients, or visitors – or their owners – sign a consent form allowing the photos to be used for publicity purposes before posting them on your website.

As I mentioned earlier, graphics are excellent tools for highlighting new services or advertising special prices for a service or deal. For example, if you own a hair salon that is offering manicures for half price, be sure to emphasize this with eye-catching graphics. Alternatively, graphics can be used to emphasize and highlight changes in prices or services. Employing graphics to accent new additions or changes helps regular visitors to quickly review the site and find these changes.

Use graphics to accentuate and add flair to a list of products or services. Encourage your visitors to want to take advantage of your special offers or try a new product. This can be accomplished with graphics that deliver a CTA (Call-To-Action), which we'll discuss in more detail later in the book. When featuring a CTA, always include a phone number, or link to another page of your site that features a contact form. This will prompt your visitor to take action on your offer immediately.

Choosing the Right Graphics for the Job

If the cost of using custom graphics is too great, or if you want to incorporate other basic images in addition to a main graphic design or logo, consider purchasing stock images. The Internet offers quite literally millions of graphics and images that can be downloaded and used by anyone. Usually, the right to feature these images can be purchased for a small fee. Sometimes, however, the owner may also require the user to note that the graphics were reprinted with permission.

As I indicated earlier, the Internet is filled with websites devoted to free and inexpensive images and graphics that you can upload to your website. One of the best websites for accomplishing this is iStockPhoto (www.istockphoto.com). Whether you purchase stock images or consult a graphic designer for custom graphics, always avoid "borrowing" copyrighted images. Posting copyrighted images without permission can lead to copyright infringement lawsuits. The penalties for copyright infringement are often quite steep, so don't "borrow" someone else's property for your own use.

Take page loading time into account when choosing graphics. Select images that are compressed into the smallest possible files. Even dial-up connections download pages five to ten times more rapidly than they did in 1995; however, most computer users expect pages to download almost instantaneously. Graphics that cause pages to load slowly can quickly become irritating, and may deter visitors from entering or returning to your site, so choose images that load quickly.

Here are a few additional do's and don'ts for graphic design. First, avoid using contrasting designs, such as black backgrounds with white text, or white backgrounds with light-colored text. Always break up blocks of text with tasteful graphics. Remember to choose a tasteful, coordinating color scheme that incorporates, rather than clashes with, photos or company logos. Banners, icons, and animated figures also help to add pizzazz and create interest. Keep essential information readable and easy to find, and use simple graphics that enhance, rather than compete with, copy content.

Pictures: Their Purpose and Their Relevance

"A picture is worth a thousand words. . . ." This old adage still applies, especially with regard to website content. Select quality pictures that enhance and emphasize your organization's services. Don't overload the website with meaningless photos, blurry shots, or unimportant details. Keep photo layouts clean and precise, and utilize pictures that help to accomplish this goal.

Use photos and designs that are relevant to your profession or business. For example, if you own an accounting corporation, consider how you can use photos and graphics to make a seemingly mundane, but very necessary service, appealing and exciting. Use graphics and photos to help meet the sometimes challenging task of demonstrating in a new and innovative way how numbers make a difference in your clients' lives.

Potential customers are also interested in family and community connections. If your business has been in the family for 100 years, emphasize this information on the corporate website. Alternatively, if you work with several family members, include photos of the family in the "About Us" section of the website. Finally, consider including photos that show your corporation or employees involved in community service projects or other positive events and activities. This will make your company even more relevant to the community and emphasize its involvement in the town's or city's everyday life.

Summing it up:

Important points to remember about graphics:

- All text and no graphics makes for a boring website. Make your site memorable with high quality graphics.

- Use graphics that reflect web content and the organization's purpose or mission.

- Check copyright details carefully before downloading graphics, or hire a consultant to design unique graphics for your website.

Important points to remember about creating visual appeal:

- Use coordinating color schemes and graphic schemes that blend, rather than clash.

- Develop a design or theme that "sells" your services or products.

Chapter Three: Website Layout

"Good order is the foundation of all things."

-     Edmund Burke

·

Now that you understand how to deliver informative content and incorporate interesting, appealing graphics, let's move on to the basics of page layout and design. Website layout is essential to the design process. Let's focus on incorporating four elements that are necessary to successfully design a web page layout. These include identity, navigation, content, and footer blocks.

Identity

A company's identity is represented by its logo or trademark. Identity, however, also incorporates much more than the simple symbol that was created to identify a business or organization. This concept also involves colors and designs used for business correspondence, advertising, and promotions. The company's identity should be evident and highly visible on every main page of the business website. This will help visitors to instantly recognize and remember key details concerning the organization's website.

Navigation

If the page is designed poorly, resulting in a confusing layout, or if the site is too difficult to navigate, visitors may leave quickly, never to return. To avoid this problem, many designers create a site map. A site map is a general navigational plan that designers use to depict the directional flow of traffic throughout a website. This strategy also offers an excellent method for featuring information or services. Visitors can access the site map and view a description of all available pages at a glance. This organized, coherent approach to design allows them to find essential information without browsing several different pages.

For example, if a potential client or customer is searching for information about the business location or hours, he or she might visit the "Contact Us" page. This page typically has the aforementioned information along with a contact form, phone number and address. Another frequently used page is "Services". This type of page might list information about the services or products available through the company. It usually also provides information about rates or fees, additional charges, or other business-specific details.

Site maps also help the designer to create a sensible, organized, layout strategy. Visitors are often likely to miss information that is not presented logically and coherently. Furthermore, they are not likely to continue browsing or consider returning to the website if they cannot find the product, service, or information for which they are searching. As a result, organized information delivery is critical to successfully presenting a product that will interest clients and visitors. That product is the service or merchandise your business is trying to sell.

Before beginning construction of the website, take a minute to sketch out a brief map of your plans on paper. Use a chart or diagram to categorize content and pages, and try to organize the content logically. Remember to make navigation as smooth as possible. Your goal is to sell yourself as an expert. As a result, you need to be able to provide important information in the few seconds that a casual visitor will spend assessing your page.

After you have done this, evaluate your efforts to organize the website's content. One helpful way to determine whether your layout design is logical and coherent is to examine the design from the perspective of a first-time visitor. Another excellent way to decide whether the content is organized is to ask a colleague, friend, or family member to search for key products or services. Ask them to evaluate whether essential information is easy to find and access. If the person has difficulty finding important data, evaluate whether re-arranging page layouts or modifying the site map might be helpful or necessary. Try to remain as objective as possible, and search for information as though you were a first-time visitor to the site.

Consider, for example, a scenario in which a photographer has just begun his or her first business venture. As a professional well acquainted with composition and design, the photographer creates a quality website that displays his or her artistic talents to maximum advantage. The website features services and fees prominently, and awards and other accolades earned by the photographer also attest to his or her expertise. If the owner fails to list the business's location and telephone number, however, clients won't be able to take advantage of that expertise.

Content

Content is paramount. Nowhere is this truer than on the Internet, where a bored reader can discard your website with the click of a mouse. Superior graphics may draw a visitor's attention for a few extra seconds. However, you will lose that visitor if you don't take advantage of those extra seconds to connect and hook him or her with high quality content.

Therefore, make that content the focal point of your website layout. Don't detract from informative copy by using distracting graphics or animation. Use the power of the written word to demonstrate conclusively that you are indeed an expert in your field. Then, use graphics and design techniques not to distract the reader, but to emphasize the site's written content. Convince visitors that they have no reason to look elsewhere for the expertise you can provide. Remember, even if your business offers the lowest prices, comparisons won't matter if your visitors don't stay long enough to read about them.

Footer Blocks

Footer blocks comprise the last, but not the least, component of successful website design and layout. These blocks of text are situated at the bottom of a web page. Usually, they contain key pieces of information that visitors will see and recall. Therefore, the content placed in these boxes should be the information you most want a reader to view and remember. Assign key pieces of information here. Include links to the website's main pages as well as copyright information, and legal or privacy notices. Always provide contact information, or at least links to the contact page, in the footer block. Most importantly, this space is ideal for a call-to-action, a "quick quote" form, or a button that prompts the visitor to click to purchase a product or contact your business.

Additionally, if your business or organization features a page on Facebook, Twitter, or another social networking site, consider including the page link and logo in the footer block. We will discuss social networking sites in more detail later in the book. For now, however, be aware that these sites are powerful tools for advertising and networking on the Internet today.

Layout Design and Readability

Creating a unique layout design isn't easy. Earning a college degree in web design and layout requires a minimum of two to four years of hard work, so don't expect to become a design guru on your first attempt. If you own a high-profile business and are trying to create a powerful website ideally optimized for search engine results, invest in the services of a professional Internet consulting company. Interview the consulting team and explain your objectives, then let them do their job. Allow them to decide which photos, graphics, and content will be most effective in promoting your business website.

Alternatively, if you are willing to spend the necessary time and energy, and are not worried about becoming a power in the Internet business world overnight, you can learn to design a web layout yourself. I will teach you some of the basic techniques used by design professionals. Then, I will show you how to incorporate these to create a quality website that features and promotes your business.

Designing a Page Layout

Begin by browsing a variety of websites. Evaluate competitor's websites, as well as other sites devoted to product sales, service provision, charity organizations, and sites for local businesses. Assess each site's use of graphics, ease of navigation, and visual appeal. Decide which sites are easier to use, and analyze which websites load faster. Consider which design layouts are most appealing, and evaluate what characteristics contribute to this appeal. Also, determine which websites feature the poorest layouts, and review how you might avoid creating similar results for your website.

Next, determine whether you want to design a totally unique layout for your website, or whether you would prefer to work from a template. If you enjoy creativity, or have had experience in designing posters or page layouts for books or scrapbooks, you might want to try designing your own layout. Take a few minutes to sketch possible designs with photos and content. Then, determine what graphics might be most useful in accentuating the copy and layout, and choose a coordinating color scheme.

If the idea of creating your own design from a sketch seems overwhelming, however, consider using a design template. Many amateur website designers, and even some professionals, choose to work with templates. These templates are easily available. Search the Internet for websites that offer free template downloads. Or, purchase a software application that contains an assortment of page templates. These applications also suggest coordinating color schemes, graphics, and background colors for web pages. Since many of these applications are rather expensive, read reviews online or discuss your needs with a design professional before purchasing an application. Don't be discouraged if the first template doesn't work as well as you thought it would. Many people often try a variety of layouts before choosing one that best meets their needs.

Balance

If you are creating your own layout, focus on developing a balanced result. An excellent way to accomplish this is to divide a sheet of paper into ninths. The result will look like a tic-tac-toe grid. Place the footer block at the bottom of the page, then start experimenting with designs. Lay out photos, text, and graphics in a variety of different combinations. Try to achieve a balanced layout. Avoid trapping blocks of text between large photos, or overwhelming your copy with bold graphics. Your goal is to create a layout that is aesthetically pleasing. Don't overwhelm the reader with a busy page filled with graphics and photos, but don't underwhelm the reader with endless blocks of monotonous copy either.

After you're satisfied with the results of your layout planning, ask a friend or colleague to critique the results.

Once you're confident you have a layout that will be visually appealing and easily navigated by visitors, review it one more time. Make sure you've remembered to include the four major components – navigation, content, identity, and footer blocks. Check to see that content, graphics, and photos flow logically. Confirm that a reader's eye will be immediately drawn to key content.

Content Readability

Use the same font for all the text included on the website. Choose a font that is easy to read. You might be tempted to select a sans-serif font to emphasize your headlines. If the chosen font is significantly different in style and appearance from that used for copy, it may actually distract the reader from the page's written content. Alternatively, if you do use the same font for headlines and copy, and the font isn't easily readable, this will also distract the visitor and discourage him or her from reading the copy. Always try to use fonts that will help to convey your message. Never use a font that forces the reader to attempt to decipher your written copy. Additionally, if you are using bullets or sidebars, use the same font you used in the rest of the site's copy.

Simply using a readable font, however, isn't enough. Content readability is another major factor in designing a website that will positively reflect your company's services or products. If you use a consulting firm, this concern is easily resolved. Most design consulting teams include, or contract with, a professional copywriter who is well-equipped to deliver the quality content necessary to help promote your website and your business.

If you are planning to do the design yourself, however, you have three options. First, you can write the content yourself. Unless you have excellent writing skills, advertising experience, and are willing to spend extra time and energy writing content, avoid the temptation. If you do decide to write your own content, proofread the copy, proof it again, and then ask an employee or family member to review it one more time.

If you don't want to do it yourself, but are trying to avoid the expense of paying someone to write the copy, consider approaching a friend, family member or employee with excellent writing skills. Be sure that person understands exactly what you want to achieve.

After the content is written, ensure that it is readable. Your goal should be to produce copy with a readability level between 10th and 12th grade. If the readability level is lower, many visitors won't find it worth reading. If the readability level is higher than this, the average reader may perceive it as too academic for casual reading. Most software applications provide review features that allow users to check a document's readability along with spell-checking and grammar-checking. Another alternative is to search online for a website that offers readability testing tools.

Some business owners opt to handle the website design and layout, and hire freelance writers to manage the content. If you choose this option, do your homework and invest in the services of a quality writer who is experienced in writing website content that is specific to your area of expertise. For example, if you are an accountant or estate attorney, consider hiring someone who is experienced in writing content about financial planning and asset protection. Quality writers, like other professionals, have areas of expertise. Don't contract with a writer who doesn't understand your business well enough to coordinate content or use technical jargon effectively.

Address your goals for readability with the writer as well. Be clear about your goals for the website. If you are designing a website for a professional research organization, for example, you may want to include research that is written in a highly technical, academic style. If, however, you are designing a medical office website featuring you and your partner, emphasize this to the writer. Explain that your objective is to encourage the average person to read and use the information, and to become your patient.

Graphics

Try to use identical or coordinating graphics each time you add new content to your website. If, for example, your site features food recipes, use the same graphic to feature that recipe each month. Always be consistent. Use this same method for adding new products or services. Use the same graphic each time you feature something new. If you do this, returning visitors will recognize and remember the graphic, and quickly see what new services or products you're offering. Remember, you may have only a few seconds to show readers that something new has been added to your site; consistent graphics will quickly help them recognize the new content and encourage them to review it.

Web designers use a variety of techniques for featuring or highlighting special content. Try each of these and see what works best for your layout. One method is to isolate the content by surrounding it with white space. White space is a term used to describe blank areas on a layout that do not contain any text or graphics.

Another strategy for highlighting content is to use bold identifying graphics or icons to draw the viewer's attention directly to that spot. Auto makers often use this method on their websites to feature new vehicle models and colors. Alternatively, designers sometimes use disproportionately large or small graphics to draw the reader's eye to important information. This technique is often distracting, though, so use it sparingly. Otherwise, the result may be a wild mismatch that distracts the reader and turns him or her away from your site.

Finally, include at least one navigation bar. One may be sufficient for dental or legal service providers. However, Internet retailers may need to use multiple navigation bars. If your website requires more than one, place it in the same location on each page.

While you are working to incorporate all of these techniques, keep in mind the reader's needs and interests. Focus on delivering the balanced, engaging graphics and quality content the viewer needs to see in order to become interested and to view you as an expert in your field. Engage the visitor, and convince him or her that the search is over. Demonstrate that your website offers exactly what he or she needs.

Summing it up:

- Keep the website readable:
- Coordinate content, graphics, photos, and white space so that the layout flows logically and looks coherent.
- Focus on aesthetics as well as readability when choosing page layouts, fonts, and graphics.
- A good website layout always incorporates these four components:
  - Identity
  - Navigation
  - Content
  - Footer Blocks

Chapter Four: Copy is King

"Think like a wise man but communicate in the language of the people."

-    William Butler Yeats

The written content, or copy, of a website is designed to initiate a conversation with site visitors. Therefore, to communicate effectively, the copywriter needs to speak the same language as the people who will be visiting the site. I don't mean this only in a literal sense. Sites designed for English-speaking people are typically written by writers who speak English fluently and understand the intricacies of language and grammar.

This concept also includes designing the content to target the intended audience. If, for example, the audience is a group of sports fans, references to classical music would probably diminish the site's credibility considerably. If, however, the website is being launched for the purpose of featuring a community arts foundation, classical music or art references would be entirely appropriate. When writing website content, always try to use the social and cultural language that anticipated visitors will best understand and appreciate.

Remember, too, that site copy is often the owner's first and only opportunity to answer a visitor's questions. If you intend to write the copy yourself, ask yourself what questions a visitor might expect to have when visiting your site. If you are working with a consulting agency, or hiring a freelance writer to create the content, be sure this information is clear to the writer before he or she begins. I've encountered a good number of disorganized clients who lacked the ability to effectively communicate what their business was all about.

Identify what information is most likely to meet a site visitor's needs. Determine which concepts are essential to that person's understanding of your business or service. Choose words and phrases that accurately describe the business's goals, and explain how the organization works to offer quality service to customers or clients. Always provide contact information so that visitors can directly contact you or your representative to resolve questions or concerns. Try to answer potential questions logically and confidently. Show your expertise in your area and let people perceive you as a guru without telling them that you are one. Otherwise, you appear egotistical and conceited. Never speak negatively about competitors.

Purpose

The content of a website is partially determined by its purpose. Different types of sites have different purposes. The main types of websites include:

- Vanity sites: These display personal biographic information, and are often created for fun or self-entertainment.

- Promotional or sales sites: These are also called brochure sites. They are used to promote a company, service or product.

- E-commerce sites: Products and sometimes services are sold through e-commerce websites through an online shopping cart.

- Current events sites: Newspapers, online journals,

and blogging sites are designed to keep the reader informed and current about news events and updates.

• Informative sites: These sites are designed to instruct the visitor on a particular topic. Examples of these include websites about hobbies, cooking or recipes, or how-to pages.

• Advocacy sites: These are used by support groups or other organizations, such as animal rescue or parenting organizations.

• Educational sites: These are used by colleges or universities, or other groups that offer distance or traditional education alternatives.

• Entertainment: These websites feature games, movies, or content that is designed to entertain.

• Registration required: Some sites are members-only sites. These are established for a wide range of purposes, including information, education, organization, and entertainment.

Consider which of these types best defines your business, service or product. Then use informative content targeted to meet the informational needs of the average user of these services. Create website content that presents this information as clearly and coherently as possible. Then you will be able to most effectively connect with and inform your visitors.

In the following sections, we'll discuss a variety of issues concerning website content and development. First, we'll talk about the various types of promotional and sales content, and how this content can best be used to communicate with visitors. Then, we'll address how to create quality web content. Finally, we'll evaluate possible strategies for optimizing content, and discuss some of the potential pitfalls in copywriting, as well as how these pitfalls can be avoided.

Types of Website Content

Different websites will require different types of content, depending on their purpose and target audience. Each of these can be used to attract visitors, but some are more effective for certain types of websites than others. Each of these has advantages, and disadvantages. The goal is to achieve a balanced effect that incorporates relevant types of copy, and utilizes the various styles to their best advantage.

Feature Articles

Feature articles include content or stories about information concerning the website's primary or secondary topics. For example, a website that focuses on distance education may include feature articles about Pell Grants, student loans, or diploma mills. Similarly, a website for a computer technology corporation might include feature articles about software development or recent innovations in the field.

Typically, feature articles aren't situated on the site's main page, or home page. Instead, designers often reserve a small section of the home page for copy containing lead-ins to these articles. These lead-ins are similar to movie trailers, encouraging readers to click the "more" link to read the remainder of the story. Usually, feature articles also include graphics and photos. These visual effects help to break up large blocks of text. They also encourage readers to finish the article. The best way to keep these articles relevant and fresh is by incorporating a blog into your site.

If you decide to write your own copy, keep feature articles focused. They should contain one, or at most two, main ideas. If you have more ideas than this, use them to write separate articles for each idea or pair of ideas. As I said earlier, when writing, always remember to keep in mind the target reader's interest and educational level. Finally, unless your website is designed to be read primarily by other experts in your professional field, avoid feature articles written in jargon. Don't try to present highly technical or complex content in a feature article; you will lose the reader's interest quickly.

Interviews and Celebrity Endorsements

Testimonials and endorsements from celebrities and experts are useful tools for selling products, services, information, and entertainment. Since your goal is to sell your site to visitors, you may elect to try using a celebrity interview or endorsement for this purpose. Remember, you want to include website content that will draw visitors in and encourage them to purchase your products or services, contribute to your organization, or visit your local store. Celebrity endorsements offer an excellent approach for accomplishing this objective.

Consider Sam's case. Sam is a skilled heart surgeon whose friend and colleague lives in another state. After this colleague devised a new technique and published books and articles about the procedure, his reputation and fame grew. People living all over the United States who needed heart surgery began contacting him, asking him to perform their operations. The colleague started referring some of these people to his skilled friend Sam. To enhance his professional reputation, Sam included an endorsement from his colleague on his website, and featured it prominently in his office as well. Visitors to Sam's website saw this endorsement, and began contacting Sam with requests to perform their surgeries.

If you have decided to post a celebrity endorsement on your website, choose someone with a positive public image. Then, interview the celebrity and ask him or her to share how your product or service has improved his or her life. Again, choose someone who has a good reputation, because such a person is well-respected, and readers are more likely to value the opinion of someone they respect. Similarly, avoid using interviews with people who have been involved in legal troubles or scandals. Any association between you and your business and a person like this may actually result in negative publicity and discourage clients or visitors from doing business with you.

Whenever possible, choose a celebrity whose reputation reflects the product or service you are trying to sell. For example, if you own a software development company that creates and sells an application to Microsoft, you may be fortunate enough to get an interview with Bill Gates. When you interview him, encourage him to share how your application benefits the computer industry, and to explain to your readers why the application is superior to other, similar products. An interview such as this will serve as a positive endorsement for the company's product. Furthermore, this will help to highlight the company's expertise in the software design and engineering industry. Other companies will take note of the applications released by the endorsed company, and may consider using those applications as well.

The best approach for incorporating interviews into website content is to use written excerpts of the conversation. Alternatively, consider embedding an audio or video file of the interview. Be sure to obtain the interviewee's permission before posting an audio or video file, or directly quoting him or her on your website.

Layout experts usually recommend featuring a brief written excerpt of the interview on the home page. Add a "Click here" icon to direct visitors to the link for reading the remainder of the interview. A similar icon could be included to allow readers to access an audio file or video of the interview.

Reviews

Reviews are similar to interviews or celebrity endorsements. This type of content, however, is written by ordinary people. People aren't paid for their reviews, so website visitors often perceive them as being more objective than interviews and endorsements.

Sometimes, people send unsolicited letters or comments about a company's products, services, or information. Many people are tempted to post only the positive information from reviews. Usually, though, experts advise the inclusion of positive reviews that also include a few negatives. If the reviews are completely positive, visitors will find it hard to believe that the reviews were written by a real person who is being objective about his or her experience.

Another way to encourage visitors to share reviews about your products and services is to include a feedback form on your website. Feedback forms encourage people to submit their feedback, or reviews. These forms often generate valuable responses that can be included in the website content.

A good review will include:

• A cost comparison of the product or service to that of other agencies or businesses

• A description of how effective or beneficial the service or product has been to the reviewer

• Honest opinions about the effectiveness of the service

• Positives and negatives of the service or product (try to use objective reviews that present both kinds of information)

• An explanation of why the service was or was not satisfactory, or what would have made the product or service better

- Comments that are relevant to your products or services (for example, no one cares whether an attorney prefers Snickers or Milky Way candy bars).

Avoid reviews that:
- Bash other websites, service providers, products, etc.
- Are written from a third person perspective
- Include content that encourages or delivers a negative overall perception of your business or organization.

Announcements and invitations

Announcements help to keep visitors, clients, and customers informed about your company's new products and services. Additionally, you can use announcements to update readers about community events in which your company will be involved. This type of content also offers an excellent venue for sharing information about special promotions or discounts. Remember to feature new product releases or business stories in the announcements section as well.

Post announcements and news stories that are informative and related to current events in your business's field of expertise. For example, a technology consulting company may publish an announcement containing a news release about a new virus threat. Similarly, the site administrator may also opt to publish an announcement about a new development in computer security. Even if the advancement was made by a rival company, the innovation is of interest to people interested in technology consulting. Always make an effort to demonstrate that your company is aware and interested in the latest advances in your field of expertise.

Additionally, post product recall notices and other information relevant to your field of expertise to which visitors should have access. Do so whether the recall involves products sold by you, a competitor, or by a related business. For instance, physicians might post notices about medications that cause serious side effects or have been recalled. Similarly, attorneys might post notices about class action lawsuits – even if they are not the attorneys directly handling the cases.

User-defined content

Readers enjoy interacting with and participating in the improvement or development of a website, product, or service. Encouraging them to share their opinions is an excellent way to encourage them to participate. To facilitate this, offer feedback forms, polls, or rating opportunities on your website. Display feedback reviews, poll results, or tally the ratings and display them on the website to remind readers that their opinions matter. Another way to accomplish this objective is through the use of star rating scales. This way, each unique site visitor has an opportunity to rate a service or product once, and offer his or her input. The result is an average rating from all visitors who choose to add their input.

Use comment forms and polls to generate valuable information. Ask readers what aspects of your area of expertise most concern them. For example, if you own an investment management firm, design your poll to discover what information would be most valuable to your readers. Offer choices about retirement savings planning, investment alternatives, college financing, or other relevant issues.

Next, post the results of the poll prominently on your site. This action allows readers to see how their concerns compared to those of other visitors. Finally, post feature stories, announcements, news stories, and other content relevant to these concerns. Remember, readers who feel that their concerns are heard and addressed become repeat customers.

Using a variety of content sources will draw readers and keep them returning. Just keep posting content that is fresh, interesting, and relevant to your readers' needs. In later chapters, I'll share with you how to optimize this content for indexing on major search engines.

Summing it up:

Website content can be divided into the following categories:

- Feature articles
- Interviews and celebrity endorsements
- Reviews
- Announcements and invitations
- User-defined content.

Chapter Five: Other Copy Concerns

Creating and Obtaining Website Content

If you've already decided to work with a marketing consulting company, the material provided in this chapter will help you gain a better understanding of the firm's decision-making process with regard to the content created for your site. The company's copywriters will generate fresh, relevant content that will keep your visitors returning to stay informed. If you're planning to write the copy yourself, however, read this information carefully so that you will develop the best possible content.

If you haven't decided yet whether to write the copy yourself, hire a freelancer, or invest in professional services, be aware that excellent writing and grammar skills are critical to the success of your efforts. If you don't enjoy writing, or aren't particularly skilled at it, don't even begin the process. Take the time, invest the money, and do your homework. Find a writer who can offer you what you want for a price you can afford.

Remember, your website will define your business's Internet presence. Most people who are 50 years of age or younger will visit your website and make a decision about whether or not to buy your products or services. They will do this before they drive by your business or even make a telephone call to inquire about your services. If your website is poorly designed, takes too long to load, or is ranked too low in search engine page results (SERPs), you will lose that potential visitor within seconds. I cannot over-emphasize to you the important role professional web design companies play in creating websites that promote your business effectively.

Many service providers make the mistake of focusing on the obvious. For example, everyone expects a veterinarian to offer caring, compassionate, professional services to each and every canine and feline that enters his or her office. Your copy should explain to readers what makes your service different. The content should answer this question: Why does your business or service stand out among competitors? Explain what makes you different from the rest, and why customers or clients will benefit more by seeing you than by choosing another professional who offers the same services.

Good writing brings the site content alive for your visitors. It will draw them in and help to evoke a multi-sensory experience that will make your site memorable. Graphics and pictures are excellent tools to help emphasize the story to potential customers, but only a wordsmith can make letters come alive on the page and tell you a story.

Remember, though, that we are talking about good copywriting. This type of writing is different from academic or research writing. It's also different from the descriptive, prosy style of literary giants such as Charles Dickens. Good copywriting should target the reading level and meet the expectations of most of the potential customers visiting the site. If you're not sure exactly what type of copy will probably appeal to most of your visitors, scan the content of competitors whose sites boast high SERPs. Jot down ideas, make comparisons, and develop ideas about what types of content you might want to incorporate into your own website. Avoid using the same content or ideas word for word. This is plagiarism, and you may soon be defending against that charge in a lawsuit.

Writing styles and strategies have changed drastically over the last 25 years. In the decades before computers became widely used, people often sat down at a desk to write, keeping handy tools like a thesaurus, dictionary, and other writing aids easily available. Today, many writers sit down at the computer and begin to type words into a word processing software application or HTML editor. They list their ideas, expound upon them, and post them on their websites or send them in emails. Unfortunately, too many fail to stop and use spell-checking tools, check grammar, or review punctuation before clicking "send."

If you prefer to sit down at your computer and start writing, remember that the Internet provides you with access to a variety of free online writing resources. These resources can mean the difference between a copy dream and a copy nightmare. Check and double-check spelling, grammar, and punctuation. Use software tools or websites that evaluate the readability and reading level of your content. Finally, share your expertise about your product or service, and explain key concepts and ideas to your visitors. Use your writing skills to communicate that expertise in a language they understand.

Strategies for Generating Website Content

Let's revisit the different types of content and examine

the sources from which they originate. First, the majority of websites include feature articles. If you're designing your own site, and are a good writer, you may want to write some feature articles about topics within your range of expertise. You may also want to explore other options, including publishing trade articles or reprinting other authors' articles with their permission.

Some sites also feature interviews or celebrity endorsements. If you have excellent communication skills and are good at interviewing people, you may decide to conduct the interviews yourself. If you do decide to conduct the interviews yourself, write very clear questions that you can reasonably expect the expert to answer. Write the questions before you hold the interview, so you don't waste the interviewee's time trying to construct questions while you are talking with him or her. Keep in mind, too, that sometimes, celebrities respond more readily to requests for email or telephone interviews than personal interviews.

If you don't know a celebrity personally, or have good media connections, you may experience considerable difficulty in trying to obtain an interview or receive a response to your written questions. Consider, for example, the rare situations in which you might encounter a celebrity at a sporting event or in a restaurant. In these situations, chances aren't high that you will have the opportunity or presence of mind to request an interview or make arrangements for an interview at that very moment. As a general rule, unless you own a high-profile business, or encounter famous people frequently, you will probably have difficulty making celebrity contacts who are willing to grant interviews.

Professional web design teams can often help with this dilemma. These teams include professional copywriters who have developed and maintained numerous celebrity contacts for precisely this purpose. Usually, outsourcing interview requests to a design team will usually result in higher-quality interviews with higher-profile people.

Sometimes, though, getting interviews from local people who are experts in their fields can be very effective for area businesses. Business owners usually don't have to resort to outsourcing to obtain an interview or endorsement from a local expert. The endorsement of local celebrities and experts is often a very effective way to attract customers within that area. For example, a local landscaping firm will probably experience greater success if its website includes endorsements offered by the area's hospital administrators or city buildings managers than if it features reviews or endorsements from celebrities living in another part of the country.

Reviews are another commonly used type of promotional copy. Contract with review bloggers, professional design teams, or customers to have your service or product reviewed. Often, review blogs will review your product or service, and then post their opinion of it with a link back to your website. Many bloggers will often do this in exchange for a free item or a service discount.

Likewise, customers or clients may agree to review your company in exchange for a discount or promotion. If you manage a hair salon or health spa, and have customers who are professional writers, consider offering her or him a free haircut or massage in exchange for a review. This kind of publicity costs little, and can be extremely effective for local businesses. If you're having difficulty generating reviews, or don't want to take time away from business operations to generate leads, outsource this task to a freelance company or design team.

Some business owners choose to link to blog sites that feature topics relevant to their services or products. In return, the bloggers post links back to the business owners' websites, generating search engine traffic. These linkbacks can sometimes be helpful. However, linkbacks sometimes have the potential to cause search engines to give low-quality indexing results for the company website. Only a design team expert or search engine optimization (SEO) specialist can really determine how beneficial or harmful a linkback is likely to be. If you are designing the site yourself, allow linkbacks cautiously, and don't hesitate to delete the links if your index rankings begin to fall.

Another alternative is to read articles, press releases, and news stories to gain leads on announcements or invitations to post on your site. Visit other websites, and search for current events or news about recent controversies, discussions, or innovations. Many business owners also work hard to maintain open lines of communication, and post

58

announcements or information about other businesses that sell their products or use their services. Business to business (B2B) lead generation, or referral, is a highly important source of revenue. As a result, informal referral agreements to share announcements, invitations, or information can be highly beneficial to both business organizations.

One other type of content that is often helpful to include is user-defined content. Encouraging comments and suggestions from customers and clients helps to make readers feel they are part of the site. This process also helps business owners to develop new and creative ideas about advertising and marketing. Consider creating a mailing list or marketing list that regularly informs repeat visitors or customers of updates, new information, marketing promotions, or sales.

Hints and Tips for Content:

Business integrity is critical for survival. If you want your customers to view you and your business as a source of reliable information, follow these rules.

Include:

• Honest opinions that aren't overbearing: Don't try to force your visitors to swallow your opinion or another person's opinion.

• Verifiable facts and information: Cite your sources whenever you use secondary information. Always credit another author's work (unless you have contracted with a freelancer who has agreed to sell the rights to their work for hire).

- Links to other reputable businesses.
- True facts or comments: If you are indeed the guru you claim to be, you have no reason to publish anything untrue on your site.

Avoid:

- Making negative comments or generating negative publicity about a competitor. This tactic doesn't make them look bad; it makes you look unethical.
- Trying to intimidate your customers, or hard-selling clients to choose your business over another competitor. This strategy will send prospective customers straight to your competitors. No one likes to be told what to do.
- Dishonest and evasive business practices. You may convince a potential customer to try a product, or draw potential buyers into your car dealership for a test drive. If you aren't honest about your policies, though, they won't trust you enough to do business with you. In fact, they may even tell others about their negative experience and turn away potential customers who will never even reach your company's site.

Summing it up:
To create or obtain content:

- Write the content yourself or outsource it.
- Use only reputable information sources.
- Research eZines, blogs, and other Internet sites for

content ideas.

- Consider outsourcing the content unless you're a very skilled writer.

Chapter Six: Call to Action

"If you don't drive your business, you will be driven out of business."

-       B.C. Forbes

So far, I've shared ways to capture an audience and techniques for layout design. I've also given you an extensive overview of general rules for developing and using website content. The next step in developing a web marketing strategy is developing and delivering a call to action, or CTA.

The call to action is the method by which you, the website owner, persuade visitors to become your customers or clients. A good CTA will help you to increase the rate at which visitors who browse your website decide to buy your product, choose your service, or subscribe to your website or newsletter. The percentage of visitors who visit your site and decide to respond to your call to action is called the conversion rate. Higher conversion rates mean more customers.

Most website visitors are unfamiliar with CTAs, and don't understand what makes them choose whether or not to purchase the product being sold by a website. (NOTE: In this context, the word product refers to the content, service, information, or merchandise being marketed by a particular website.) Visitors usually are either completely uninterested in your product or somewhat interested in what you're marketing. Your goal as a web designer should be to create a CTA that will encourage those who are interested in your product to become consumers of that product.

The purpose of this chapter is to help you learn to identify CTAs that are commonly used by web designers to increase conversion rates. By reading this chapter, you'll learn to recognize and critique CTAs, and to find ways to implement them in your own website.

In this chapter, we'll discuss:
- The purposes of a website
- Types of desired actions
- Steps to an effective call to action.

Purposes of a Website

In chapter 4, you learned that different types of websites have different purposes. The goal of each of these is to encourage or induce a visitor to proceed with some form of action. Now, let's consider these types of websites and their purposes more fully.

- Vanity site

The purpose of a vanity site is to provide personal information, often biographical or career-related. Many celebrities host vanity sites to promote their career and to provide information about their movies, books, songs, or accomplishments. They often update these pages by commenting about their daily routine or a special event on a sidebar column, which can be programmed to pull in feeds from sites like Facebook and Twitter. Most vanity sites also include options for fans to sign up for and receive regular newsletter updates as well.

- Promotional and sales sites

These sites are designed to sell products, promote services, or generate contact leads. If you've ever purchased something or submitted requests for an insurance quote online, you've visited a promotional or sales site. The primary goal of these sites is conversion. The site owner wants the visitor to buy a product or service, or make a direct contact for that purpose.

- Current events sites

These websites host online magazines, journals, newspapers, and circulars. The goal of these sites is to encourage readers to subscribe and read the latest news about business, sports, professional events, or world events online. Current events sites are designed to educate readers.

- Informational sites

Information sites provide information on an endless variety of topics. Hobby pages, tax tip sites, and photography instructional pages are all examples of informational sites. Some of these hobby pages are hosted by individuals who want to promote their hobbies. Others are sponsored by corporations who create links to their corporate pages, hoping that visitors will also stop by their Internet store and make a purchase.

- Advocacy sites

These sites are designed to persuade readers to adopt their viewpoints. Websites for religious organizations, political parties, animal rights leagues, and support groups are all examples of advocacy sites. Usually, these sites don't issue a CTA for a purchase. Instead, the designer's goal is to persuade readers to support the organization's cause by some other means. This may include donations, participation in fund-raising events, signing petitions, or attending meetings.

- Instructional sites

Instructional websites are primarily how-to sites designed for people who want to tackle a project or learn a new skill. These sites contain clear step-by-step instructions for completing tasks.

- Registration required sites

Some sites require registration so that they can control, or moderate, comments made by users regarding certain subjects on forums or message boards. Others require registration as part of a process in which they claim to deliver proprietary information about curing a health problem or getting a work-at-home job.

These sites require users to enter email addresses, which are often used to provide marketing information about specialty products or services on a daily or weekly basis. Typically, users are barraged by marketing emails until they request to be removed from the site's mailing list. This type of marketing rarely works and can be very annoying to visitors.

- Entertainment sites

These sites are designed to entertain. Games, movie sites, trivia sites, and gossip pages are designed to entertain readers so that they will continue returning to the site to learn more.

To summarize, every website has a purpose. The purpose of each website is the same: to encourage the visitor to respond to a call to action. Different types of sites, however, call for different actions. These actions include:

Buying

If your website markets a certain product, your goal should be to deliver a call to action that will convert your viewer to a customer. This product may be tangible merchandise, consulting services, healthcare, or legal services. Develop your sales pitch, and then use your website to deliver that pitch effectively with a call to action, or CTA.

Support

Advocacy sites issue a CTA for viewers to support their cause. They do this by encouraging viewers to become actively engaged in promoting the cause.

Subscribe

Many informational and instructional websites issue a CTA to subscribe to their websites. People don't want to waste their time subscribing to meaningless sites, though. Therefore, in order to persuade people to subscribe to your site, you will need to demonstrate why the subscription will benefit the visitor. Otherwise, your CTA will not be effective.

Inform

Although your primary goal is to inform your visitor, you also want him or her to continue reading the rest of the website. A CTA for an informational site often involves capturing the reader's interest on the front page and persuading him or her to move on to the remaining pages by clicking to read more.

All websites use at least one CTA. Many use multiple CTAs to persuade readers to act. Furthermore, different CTAs appeal to different visitors for different reasons. For example, a web marketing company may issue a CTA encouraging visitors to begin by accepting a free consultation. Interested visitors are often motivated to respond to an offer for a free cost estimate for technology services.

This same site, however, may also issue a CTA to visitors to learn more about current events in the technology industry. Readers who respond to the second CTA may also continue to explore the site and take advantage of the free consultation featured with the first CTA as well. In addition to these services, the site will also market web design services.

Creating an Effective Call to Action

Now that you understand the purpose of a call to action, or CTA, it's time to learn how to effectively implement one on your website. First, encourage the action in language that your visitor understands. Use terms like buy, subscribe, view, or donate.

Next, establish a sense of urgency that encourages your readers to act now. Use time-sensitive content that encourages a visitor to take action now in order to secure a bargain price, make a donation that will save an acre of rain forest before it's too late, or receive valuable information that will help him or her today.

Some sites use "click here" or "read more" to deliver a CTA, but these CTAs don't carry a sense of urgency. While they may be helpful for informational sites, they do not encourage visitors to complete a buying action promptly. When you deliver a CTA that lacks immediacy, visitors are more likely to put off answering your call. As a result, less urgent calls that do not encourage a prompt decision are much less likely to be answered. These CTAs are less likely to increase conversion rates than those that encourage an immediate response.

Deliver your call to action with minimal text. At most, use a few lines of text, or a couple of sentences that emphasize and describe the call to action. Encourage readers directly with words like "you" and "your." Demonstrate the benefits of your product or service first, and then present the offer. Never push the product directly.

For instance, a computer technology company's website might encourage visitors in the following manner: "Avoid endless hours spent recovering lost data. Get FREE identity theft protection software by ordering your virus protection program upgrade within the next 24 hours!"

Color

Use graphics and colors that stand out and call the

reader's attention directly to the CTA. You are most likely to achieve this objective by using contrasting colors and graphics because they stand out and call the reader's attention to the CTA. Different colors send different messages to visitors, so emphasize your CTA by taking advantage of the messages these colors send.

For example, red is often associated with danger signs or warning signals, while green is often associated with establishing trust, and may be ideal for use in testimonials, interviews, or reviews. Blue is calming and does not usually draw attention, but yellow is very noticeable and draws attention. Orange is a cheerful color, but may sometimes be interpreted as indicative of aggression.

Size

Size also matters. Use graphics that are larger than the text, but maintain a balance, or the graphics will completely overwhelm textual content and dominate the page. You want to draw the reader without screaming at him or her to CLICK THE BUTTON. The best way to choose the size of your graphics in a CTA is by experimentation. Enlarge or shrink the graphics, and review the results before finalizing the size.

Location

Always consider location, location, and location. Position your CTA so that it is surrounded by white space or smaller text. Situate the CTA on the front page of the website so that it calls out to the visitor as soon as he or she reaches your site. Place it in the upper half of the page, and centralize the location whenever feasible. You may have only seconds to get the reader's attention and draw him or her in, so locate the CTA where it will be visible as soon as the page begins to load.

Display the primary CTA on all pages of your website. Ideally, it should be situated in approximately the same location on all pages. That way, when the viewer is ready to make his or her decision to become a customer, he or she is already conditioned to look in a certain spot.

Remember to keep it simple. Multiple CTAs can be effective, if they work together in unison and don't compete for the reader's attention. Consider the example of the computer technology website. Imagine how frustrated a website visitor might become if he or she was encouraged to download a virus protection program in order to get free identity theft protection, but had to go to another page to read the offer before downloading the programs. Then, once the download button was clicked, the reader was informed that first he or she had to register and subscribe to the site to get the special offer. In this case, competing CTAs would be more likely to deter than attract customers.

Also, consider including bonuses or freebies as part of your CTA. For example, if you offer estate planning services, incorporate free consultations, extra copies of a will, or free will revisions with the establishment of a living trust or other service. When the customer returns for a free will revision, he or she may also need other legal services at the time. Most importantly, you will have established yourself in that customer's mind as an essential legal resource should a future need for legal services arise.

Summing it up

In this chapter, we've reviewed:

* The purposes of a website:
  • Vanity
  • Promotion or sales
  • Current events and news
  • Informational
  • Advocacy
  • Instructional
  • Registration required
  • Entertainment
* Actions desired from website visitors:
  • Buy
  • Support
  • Subscribe
  • Inform
* Steps for designing a CTA:
  • Encourage the action
  • Establish urgency for completing the action
  • Use colors to emphasize the CTA – consider color contrasts and meanings
  • Size matters – make visitors notice the CTA
  • Consider location, location, and location – position

CTAs so the reader finds them

- Keep it simple – avoid competing CTAs
- Continuity – put the same CTA on every page in similar locations
- Bonuses and freebies – offer extras that encourage the reader to return.

Chapter Seven: Search Engine Marketing

"Thousands of people were producing new websites every day. We were just trying to take all that stuff and organize it to make it useful."

- David Pilo

In previous chapters, we've discussed how to create aesthetically pleasing websites that appeal to visitors and are filled with relevant, captivating content. We've reviewed content, graphics, and design layout. I shared how to create and deliver a call to action. Now that you've learned how to create an outstanding business site, you need to discover how to draw traffic to your new site.

Stop for a moment and consider how you search for content on the Internet. Unless you know the exact URL of the website, you probably open your preferred web browser and enter the name of a favorite search engine. You type in some keywords and try to find the information you are seeking. If this doesn't work, you try other, similar keywords and scan through the results the search engine returns.

But how does the search engine find the results you want? In this chapter, we'll discuss how that occurs. Usually, getting a search engine to list your website in its search results involves a little luck, a little art, and a little science.

Most people rarely look beyond the first page or two of results. Therefore, making the first page or two of results is essential in drawing traffic to your website. You may do this either by purchasing an ad on the search engine's front page results, or by optimizing your content for indexing by search engines.

Use one of these three methods to be successful in search engine marketing:
- Organic search results
- Pay-per-click search results

- Link building.

Organic Search Engine Optimization

Organic, or natural, search engine optimization involves using keywords and keyword phrases to make a website easy to find on a search engine's result page (SERP). These keywords, together with tags and meta tags, are "found" and indexed by search engines. Websites with the most relevant and easily located keywords are ranked higher than sites with less pertinent keywords or phrases.

A wide variety of search engines are available for use. Only a few, however, are truly popular, and a few more are somewhat popular. All of them use "spiders" to rank search results. These spiders are lines of code that are programmed to crawl across indexed pages, spotting and counting keywords. An engine's SERP results are determined by the number of relevant keywords and the location of these words on the site's pages.

Each page on a website also has a unique Internet address. Most sites include a home page, several pages of content, a summary page, and a page for links to other sites. Search engine spiders travel rapidly over the page searching for relevant keywords, phrases, and links. The spiders then relay this information to the search engine so that the pages can be indexed and ranked.

Use one keyword phrase for each web page, but don't overuse that phrase. If the information is too repetitive, the spider may "blacklist" your website. This means that your site may be ranked much lower on the SERP or removed altogether.

Develop a plan for optimizing organic search results by using the following:

Tags

Effective search engine optimization incorporates the use of three types of tags: HTML tags, meta description tags, and meta keyword tags. As with a page's Internet address, each page also requires a set of unique tags. Let's examine each type of tag more closely:

HTML Title Tags

Each page of code has a title tag. This is the information you see in the browser window at the very top – the descriptor for the web page. It appears like this: "This is the Title of the Page." Keep these rules in mind when creating a title tag:

• The title is displayed when someone bookmarks a page. Keep the title short and word it wisely so that visitors do not have to change the title when bookmarking it to remember what information the site contains.

• Use upper- and lower-case letters; titles are displayed exactly as they are entered.

• Spiders see the title page first. Use the page's keyword phrase in the title if possible so that the spider will easily identify the page's subject.

• Use unique title pages for every indexed page.

• Create a title page for the site's home page that incorporates the organization's name. Don't use generic titles that don't identify the website's purpose.

- Use keyword phrases in logical sentences. Don't just string phrases together.

- Keep the title tag shorter than 65 characters; otherwise, the search engine may cut it off.

Meta Description Tags

These tags are used on the SERP. The SERP returns a list containing relevant sites, brief descriptions of these sites, and their Internet addresses. This brief description is the page's meta description tag. For your site's homepage, create a meta description tag that briefly describes your entire website. Alternatively, use this tag to describe the content of the main page in 170 characters or less. (If you write longer descriptions, the search engine will truncate your description after the first 170 characters).

The code for a meta description tag appears like this: <meta name="description" content="This is the brief description of the page's contents." >

Meta Keyword Tags

Meta keyword tags are not visible anywhere on the website or SERP. These tags are the keywords or keyword phrases used in each page's content. Ideally, these should be used only once on the main page, and a unique set of phrases should be used for each additional page. The keywords and keyword phrases should be listed in descending order of importance and relevance.

The meta keyword tag line looks like this: <meta

name="keywords" content="keywords,keywords,keywords, keyword phrase,keyword phrase">.

Some web design experts do not believe meta keyword tags are indexed at all by search engines. Others believe that search engines rely heavily on this information. Even though there is some uncertainty about this, most believe it is best to include this information, just in case.

Text Navigation

The term "text navigation" describes the set of text-based links that connect one page to another within a website. For example, the "about us" text in a footer block allows visitors to click directly on that text and be taken to a page that describes the website or organization. Another way to use text navigation is for linking pages of content or feature articles.

Search engine spiders use text navigation to move from one page to another more rapidly. To take full advantage of this, create text-based links that contain the keywords and keyword phrases researched and used in the page's content. Using text navigation on the page benefits search engine spiders. It is also very helpful to human site visitors.

Site Maps

A site map can best be explained as a text-based road map of the website's layout. Site maps allow users to see the overall design and pattern for the layout of the site's pages. Experienced Internet surfers often go directly to a site map to scan the overall layout of the site rather than visiting the website page by page. Spiders also use site maps for search engine indexing and page ranking.

Navigation Organization

Categorization is another important aspect of site organization. For example, universities may categorize their educational offerings by undergraduate, graduate, and postgraduate course work. They may use these and other categorizations to make sense of the information they provide on their site.

Similarly, Internet commerce sites like eBay offer product search categories, information categories, communication categories, and forum categories. To categorize your site effectively, use a logical system for organization. Further, confirm that everything featured on your site is included in the categorical structure so that something isn't inadvertently omitted from the organization chart. When you develop your system, keep the links on the chart connected, so that users can travel from page to page using the text navigation links provided on each page. If your visitor has to return to the home page after each search, he or she may quickly become frustrated.

Review the sites of competing organizations whose websites are indexed highly on the SERP. Take special note of their use of navigation organization and navigation text. Consider patterning your organizational system similarly.

Directory Submission

The next step in search engine marketing is to submit

your website to major website directories and search engine directories. These directories function much like the yellow pages section of the telephone book. Most of the larger search engines, including Google, Yahoo, and AOL Search, use a directory known as the Open Directory Project. The URL for this free service is http://www.dmoz.org. One other advantage of using the Open Directory Project is that search engines view this as an indication of a reputable site, which also helps boost your SERP ranking.

Although this site updates listings on a weekly basis, having your site approved may take weeks or months. Using this free service, however, can greatly increase the number of unique visitors to your site. If you have difficulty selecting a category for your site, submit your information to what you believe to be the closest logical choice. Project staff will edit the category or other information as needed.

Consider registering the physical location of your company or organization with search engines as well. For example, Google Maps offers free registration and also provides website administrators with valuable feedback about how people are locating their websites. This process is no more difficult than making sure your company is listed in the yellow pages of the local phone book.

Decide whether to use a free service such as Open Directory Project, or spend a minimum of $50 for expedited review through a paid directory site. Additionally, you can opt to pay a one-time fee for these services, or choose to pay annually for the listing. These sites are easy to find; just search the keywords "website directories" and you'll get hundreds of results.

Avoid using search engine optimization (SEO) or search engine marketing (SEM) firms that claim to use scripts to instantly rank your website high on SERPs. These scripted submissions are often blacklisted by reputable directories that manually review websites.

This is because the scripts submit information without regard to proper category guidelines established by the directory. Another problem is that sometimes these scripts result in multiple submissions from the same URL to these directories. You are much more likely to spend money remedying the damage caused by SEO scripts than spending the money earned from using them.

After you've completed these steps, wait for the results. It may take weeks or even months for site traffic to increase noticeably. If the process doesn't work right away, don't assume you did something wrong and start making huge changes. If, however, a reasonable time passes and you don't notice any increase, start making one small change at a time to tweak the results.

Link Building

A third type of search engine marketing is link building, also known as linkbacks, backlinks, or link popularity. Link building is time-consuming and can be frustrating, but it is very necessary. Search engine spiders look for links, so credible links are extremely important.

If you want your company's name to be easily recognized and seen, you have to link to other websites. Most marketing experts recognize that, no matter how much money you spend on advertising, business to business marketing is still critical for business success. Link building increases your SERP ranking, and it also increases your visibility on other websites. If you link to the right websites, visitors to those sites will see your links and click on them.

Three different types of links will help to accomplish this. Links on your sites to other web pages, or links on other web pages to your site, are most useful and most highly regarded by search engine spiders. You can also use reciprocal links, wherein you link to a website and that website links back to yours, but these aren't as beneficial or highly regarded by spiders.

Remember: If your site is well-designed and you demonstrate yourself to be an expert in your field, other site owners will want to link to your site. Credibility is always the key. If you want to be seen as a reputable expert, link your site to those operated by others who are respected experts in their fields. Don't link to disreputable or bizarre sites that may cause you or your business to be perceived negatively.

Here are some potential sources for developing linkbacks:

Article Directories
Submit article content to reputable article directories like Ezine Articles or GoArticles. At the bottom of the article, include a brief history of your expertise on this subject, and encourage the reader to "Visit www.mywebsite.com

for more innovative ideas on (article topic)." This service is free, and article directories draw new readers every day. Take advantage of free publicity.

Forums and Groups

Register at forums or discussion groups that focus on your topic of expertise, and post regularly. Post relevant answers and comments that are worth reading, and occasionally include a link to your website when posting, as well as a brief history of your expertise. You don't have to use perfect punctuation and grammar, but don't use slang, sloppy writing techniques, or excessive, unnecessary jargon. If your reader finds your comment or information helpful and informative, he or she is much more likely to click your link to see what else you have to say than if you posted meaningless responses with links to your website.

Affiliate Programs

These are often used in e-commerce to help encourage visitors to link to your website. They receive a profit of any sales generated as a result of their link, and you receive additional exposure. Screen requests carefully and only allow links from reputable websites. If these websites have unethical business practices or don't generate much traffic, you aren't likely to benefit from permitting these websites to post affiliate links to your site.

Community Resources

Take advantage of local community resources to

promote your business's or organization's website. Become a member of the Better Business Bureau and keep your record in good standing. Additionally, register your business with the local Chamber of Commerce, and add your site's link to the local community library resource page. These free services all help to promote your organization in the local business arena.

Friends and Family

Encourage friends and family members to post comments and reviews on your website. Include a link to your website in personal emails as well. Everyone likes to brag a little about the expert in his or her family, and you can quickly become that expert. Enjoy the free publicity that family and friends can generate.

Business Relationships

Make business connections with businesses and organizations that are related to, but not in competition with, yours. For example, if you own a hobby store, consider linking to credible instructional sites that offer how-to information to your customers. Alternatively, crafters' clubs or other hobby organizations may request to place a link to your page on their website so that members can access supplies easily.

Reviews

Offer reviews at Amazon.com, ePinions.com, and other

popular review sites. Review products and services related to your organization, or that you have personally used. Include positives, negatives, and serious problems with the product or service. Remember, if you "flame" someone with seriously negative feedback, he or she is likely to return that favor.

Always try to provide sincere, engaging content that is meaningful to the reader. When possible, include a link to your website with your review. This technique can generate more leads than you might expect.

Pay-Per-Click Advertising

Pay-per-click advertising is another form of search engine marketing. Google's AdWords is quite frankly the only option worth considering. This paid service can be pricey, so consider your advertising budget before taking the plunge. The price per click increases with the popularity of the keyword or keyword phrase chosen, so remember that the best ads will also be the most expensive.

PPC campaigns feature banners or links listed on the SERP that are designed to promote your site and increase its visibility. Each time a viewer sees a search results page, your ad or link may appear either at the top of the page or in a sidebar to the right of the results. Whenever your website makes the PPC list on a search and a viewer clicks on your website link, you pay a price for that click.

Most PPC campaigns run for a specific time frame. They may run nationally or only within a certain geographic area.

This is especially helpful for a local corporation or service organization working to draw customers that live within a certain radius of their physical location.

Consider time and budget when planning your ad. Set a daily budget, and determine how much money you are willing to pay per click. After visitors have clicked your ad enough times to use up the money in your daily budget, the ad results will be suspended for that day. On some days, or if you have a very small budget, you might hit the limit early in the day. Therefore, your ad might become inactive long before peak surfing hours. On other days, however, you might not hit the limit all day. Try to plan to run your ad during a time when the majority of your visitors are likely to be surfing.

After you've set a budget, create your ad using keyword or keyword phrases. If you have no idea where to start, Google offers a free program designed to help generate keywords used for advertising. After you've completed the ad, estimate the average number of clicks – and the cost – you can expect to generate each day. Enter billing information, choose a start date, and wait for the ad to run.

Some people decide to attempt to run PPC campaigns themselves, while others would prefer to hire an agency to manage the campaign. If you choose to use an agency, take your time and do your research. Don't just choose the first company you see that offers consistent number one results. Check each company's reputation and select a firm that offers proof of consistently delivering good marketing results. Google AdWords is a very complex system that takes a lot of time to master. The cost a pro charges to manage your campaign usually pays for itself quite quickly.

Summing it up

Now you've learned more about search engine marketing and search engine optimization. Remember these important concepts:

Organic SEO

- Use title tags, meta description tags, and meta keyword tags.
- Implement text navigation.
- Create a site map.
- Use navigation organization techniques to help visitors and search engines make sense of your website.
- Choose between free directory submission resources and paid directory submission resources.
- Link building is a time-consuming yet important part of building SEO traction.
- Link Building
- Take advantage of article directories.
- Register and participate in forums and discussion groups.
- Consider participating in affiliate programs.
- Ask friends and family to help spread the word.
- Create and maintain good business relationships with related companies.
- Write product and service reviews.

Pay-Per-Click (PPC) Campaigns

- Obtain quicker advertising results – for a price.
- Establish a budget and stick to it.
- Avoid SEM companies that promise miraculous results.

Chapter Eight: Browser Considerations

"If you have a website, it makes your small business look big."

- Natalie Sequera

A variety of Internet browsers are available for surfing the web, including Mozilla Firefox, Google Chrome, Safari, and Internet Explorer. The same website, when accessed by different browsers, may look slightly different. This occurs because every browser's coding and operating mechanisms are slightly different. For example, fonts may appear larger or smaller, or lines may appear off-center, depending on which browser a visitor is using.

No one knows exactly which browser is most popular. Some reports indicate that at least 50 percent of all Internet users prefer Firefox. Others state that Internet Explorer is most popular. As a result, good website developers seek to eliminate as many potential incompatibility problems as they can. Completely eliminating every possible change that may occur as a result of using different browsers may be impossible. You should, however, try to minimize the visual differences as much as possible. Remember, most casual Internet surfers aren't aware of possible browser compatibility issues. Many visitors who see the visual results of coding variations will simply think that your website wasn't carefully proofread or coded. This perception certainly would not enhance your status as an expert with these visitors!

Consider, for example, the case of a website that is maintained by a computer programming or repair service. Visitors to the website might believe that the owners of that business aren't concerned enough about their company to produce a quality site. Worse, they might believe that the owners fail to pay careful attention to details. People are much less likely to trust their Internet security to a business that doesn't appear to pay attention to details.

Web design companies are well-informed about browser incompatibilities and how to fix these problems. Furthermore, these businesses have the necessary resources to review and change coding to make it as compatible as possible with as many browsers as possible. If you're designing your own website, however, several free Internet programs are available for helping designers check browser compatibility and advise them of any potential problems. These programs won't find every coding issue, though. Furthermore, if there are problems, the fix is up to you if you're doing it all yourself.

JavaScript vs. Java

Learning the difference between JavaScript and Java programming is also important. JavaScript is a scripting language used inside an HTML code to enhance a web page. In comparison, Java is similar to C and C++ programming. Programmers use it to create small programs called applets that run an application on a web page. For instance, many game sites use Java to run games programs. Games are run independently on a web page accessed by opening an Internet browser window. After the page loads, the Java applet initiates its programmed function. These applets are often blocked by business networks because of security and productivity concerns.

Many web designers use JavaScript instead. These scripts promote increased flexibility and design choice, and cause a web page to be more interactive with visitors. Some browsers may be configured to automatically disable JavaScript. Design experts often recommend the use of JavaScript for the purpose of detecting the browser used by the visitor. Upon detection, the script then redirects the browser so that it will become fully functional with the website being accessed.

Learning about and understanding the differences between browsers, as well as the use of HTML coding and JavaScript, can be time-consuming and confusing. If you don't already have some expertise in this area, you may want to consider consulting a team of design experts. They can utilize your design layout preferences and content to create a fully functional website that avoids these incompatibility issues and coding problems.

Summing it up:

Browser Conversion:

• Focus on overall compatibility for web browsers rather than optimizing the HTML coding for only one browser.

• Learn when to use JavaScript and when to use Java.

Chapter Nine: Social Networking

"We are advertis'd by our loving friends."

-       William Shakespeare

Social networking sites can be a helpful way to get free advertising through your friends and family. They link people from every country of the world together, creating social groups that keep in touch and communicate about important issues and ideas. These sites can also be very helpful in promoting a business. People join social networking sites for a variety of reasons, including:

- Meeting new people, staying in touch with family and friends, or reuniting with classmates or relatives
- Keeping a virtual journal or blog to share their story with others
- Finding other people who are interested in a particular subject or hobby
- Marketing and advertising their businesses.

Social networking sites allow people of all ages to participate and discuss information. While these sites are most popular with younger generations, a high percentage of more mature adults also join these sites. Social networking sites are also exponentially growing credibility in the business world. This is because they allow companies to create a public profile and a way for unlimited numbers of potential clients to interact. They also distribute information or advertise promotions and discounts without spending money on advertising. Business owners can use these sites to boost clientele, increase public awareness about the business, and advertise.

There's another very important aspect of social networking for business that ties in with our chapter about SEO. It's becoming increasingly apparent that search engines' algorithms are making social networking participation an important part of the equation. The more followers you have and the more you use social networking, the more it seems to increase your rankings.

This chapter will discuss:

- The benefits of social networking sites, including Facebook, LinkedIn, and Twitter
- Blogging and newsletters
- MySpace (and reasons to avoid using MySpace for business purposes)
- The process of creating enticing social networking profiles for your business.

Facebook, Twitter, and LinkedIn

Many employers are "pre-screening" job applicants and "reviewing" employees online by using search engines to locate information. They do this because they have found this approach to be helpful in the hiring process. Prospective customers are using a similar process to "pre-screen" businesses before calling, walking into an organization's physical location (if one is available), or asking friends or family for a referral or recommendation. Social networking sites offer business owners an ideal venue for creating an online presence that favorably advertises their services or products to potential customers researching the business online.

These social networking sites offer businesses a chance to build a rapport with potential customers by creating a virtual hub where both business and client can interact. The means for such an effective form of marketing that's inexpensive and offers a huge ROI has never been seen before. We're at the forefront of this phenomenon, so learn about it now, get your business involved, and reap the benefits!

Facebook

Facebook was developed by Harvard student Mark Zuckerberg while still living and working in the college dormitory. This site is incredibly popular with tens of millions of individuals, groups, and businesses worldwide. It allows each user to create a profile and determine whether that profile will be public or private. Now Facebook offers "Fan" pages for businesses and the ability to integrate code into your website to "Like" things that will then display on the fan's profile.

Users can also upload profile photos, videos, or other links, subscribe to newsfeeds, and keep calendars for birthdays and important events. They can join groups or causes and suggest those groups to friends. Profile users can add friends by directly searching for other Facebook users. Alternatively, they can upload their entire email address book and instruct Facebook to search for users by email address.

Facebook also offers users the option of mobile access

and SMS messaging. This allows them to be notified instantly of a change in a friend's (or business's) status. Business owners can take advantage of this option to send customer "friends" a daily business quote or recent news in the industry. Many owners also add a link, photo, or video to this daily comment, and encourage their Facebook friends to visit the business website regularly.

Facebook can be incredibly useful to business owners who want to show a more personal side of their business and gain fans. It's also a helpful tool for those interested in making professional contacts or drawing visitors to their company websites. Many business owners try to accomplish both of these goals simultaneously.

If you link your professional website to your Facebook fan page, remember that visitors will be likely to visit both. If you have a superb website, and your Facebook profile is extremely professional as well, visitors looking for a "human" side of the business may be disappointed. Try to keep your Facebook profile personable and positive, and remain approachable to potential customers and clients who may just want to say hello or ask about your favorite NBA team. Remember, sharing your knowledge is ok, but don't turn off visitors by being too professional.

Twitter

This social networking site offers almost endless potential for free mass marketing. Twitter allows users to "micro-blog," in 140 characters or less, about anything imaginable. People "tweet" about random thoughts, "re-tweet" what another "tweeter" posted, link to interesting articles, announce sales or special events … the opportunities are endless. Even though it often seems that these comments are inconsequential or even meaningless, they can have surprising effects. Many seemingly meaningless "tweets" get thousands of views, and the people who make these hits often become followers of that "tweeter."

Ultimately, as a business owner you'll set up your Twitter account and "follow" people you're interested in with the hope that they'll follow you back. You'll get more followers by posting a link to your Twitter profile on your website, in your email, on your business card, or any other place that will drive traffic. I recommend tweeting at least once per day, but keep in mind that over-tweeting may annoy followers and they can just as easily un-follow you with the click of a link.

Before you become overwhelmed by the prospect of tweeting to potentially thousands (or millions in some cases) of people each day, consider these ideas:

• Small but witty observations can result in a re-tweet, new followers, and potentially, new customers.

• Engaging with other tweeters can start an informal dialogue that can lead to a business relationship. To talk with other tweeters use the "@" before the Twitter profile name. For example, mine is jDaz, so your tweet might say, "@jdaz how's the weather in arizona today?".

• Using the "#" next to a word will allow other tweeters

to search topics and potentially follow you. For example, a tweet might say, "here's some #webdesign advice – make sure you link it to twitter!".

Tweeters can also market local businesses by using Twitter for promotional purposes. They can encourage followers to post a tweet to their profile to get a discount on an order or service. Alternatively, business owners can use Twitter to connect to customers by posting a tweet that draws attention to the business's product or service. Many people like to feel connected, and having a Twitter page is a great way to do this without spending hours each day conversing with clients and customers.

For example, if you have a pet grooming business with hundreds of clients, you don't have time to respond to each one every day. Perhaps a new shampoo or coat treatment is being sold that prevents or treats skin problems. If you tweet about this, all of your followers will see this, and many of them will call to set an extra appointment to have their favorite pooch pampered.

Another benefit of having Twitter followers is that you will be able to stay updated on the kinds of information, products, and services that are relevant to your customers. If you own an investment consulting business, and notice several followers tweeting their concerns about how the latest congressional bill may affect the economy, consider posting a feature article on your company's website – and linking to it with Twitter.

LinkedIn

This social networking site is different from Facebook and Twitter in that LinkedIn primarily focuses on business networking. Users can select a free personal account or create a premium business profile for a fee. Premium accounts are primarily used by job seekers. Business owners usually find it most cost-effective to take advantage of the free advertising provided with the personal profiles.

LinkedIn allows business owners to help define their places in the business world. Owners can post their business resumes and company information online, and link with colleagues, current and former employees. They can also cultivate other business contacts that will be advantageous to their companies. Owners can connect with everyone they know, and be seen by everyone who needs to see them.

LinkedIn can also be used to make connections based on relationship degrees. Make "first degree" connections with personal contacts, and "second degree" connections with people who know your personal contacts. This will create a ripple effect, and generate credible referrals through contacts and contacts of contacts. Choose first degree contacts wisely, and only create these relationships with people who show business integrity, and in whom you are confident.

LinkedIn also offers users the benefit of free lead generation. The immediate contacts of your first degree contacts will locate people in whom their friends trust – you – and turn to you for business or services. Another way to generate leads is to make closer contacts with second degree connections.

For example, if you own a fabric store at a physical location, you may notice that a second degree connection specializes in delivering certain fabrics at a wholesale price. By contacting this connection, you can make a closer business connection, and probably get a sizable discount on fabrics, as well as other supplies, through this connection.

Even better, making a closer contact with this connection will help you develop other second degree connections as well. This may increase revenue and may offer savings opportunities, as well as generate business leads, customers, and traffic to your website. Furthermore, your profile will be visible to other people searching for fabric stores in your location. Potential customers will see you – and so will potential business contacts who want to offer you deals on pricing and supplies.

MySpace

MySpace was synonymous with social networking when it launched. It has since waned in popularity and is now used primarily by children for social interaction amongst themselves. Simply put, unless you're in the entertainment field, MySpace is not a social networking site that's useful for companies and businesses. If you own a club, restaurant, or music promotion business, this may be helpful. Generally speaking, Twitter, Facebook, and LinkedIn offer better options for business networking.

Creating your Social Networking Profile

When creating a profile for your business, consider your business image. You want to be respected and highly regarded, so don't create a profile that shows you as a wild and crazy party animal. Don't share information about yourself that you don't want to be associated with your business.

As a general rule, if you wouldn't want your grandmother to know the information, don't post it online. People will search for information about you if they have read your profile and are curious, and they will find the negative as well as the positive information. Furthermore, they will focus on the negative.

Make your profile informative. Share personal hobbies, vacation preferences, or discuss your participation in local community and charity events. Post information about your education and business experiences. Share information that shows your personality and business in a positive light, and be sure to include any details that are relevant to your business.

Remember, though, that your profile is accessible to everyone, so consider your privacy. You may not mind having family and friends know the name of your daughter's preschool, but you may not want everyone to know that your son walks home from elementary school every day. Keep safety in mind, and be prudent about what you post on the Internet.

Choose a photo that shows you at your best. Wear

business or business casual dress, and look like the business professional you want clients to see. Select an image that is slightly more casual than the photo on your professional site, but don't overdo it. Unless you're a professional model, you probably won't want to post a photo of yourself relaxing at the beach.

Blogging

The term "blog" is an abbreviation for "web log." Blogs are a sort of online diary or journal in which people can share their thoughts, feelings, and observations. Many sites host blog pages. Registration is usually free, and users can add a brief profile. Creating a blog page is very easy; users just choose a layout template, upload pictures, and start writing.

If the host site offers a design similar to your business website's layout, and if you have design skills, you may be able to design a blog site that appears very similar to your website. Many business owners link their blog site to their business website. This allows search engine spiders to locate keywords that you use while writing your blogs, especially if you tag those keywords. This will also help your ranking and SERP. An even more convenient option is to consult with a web design company to integrate a page on your website that functions as a blogging portal. If you choose this route, you will maintain complete control over both your business site and your blog site.

When you blog, you can choose at what date and time

your blog will be posted. If you want your blog to appear on Monday morning at the start of business, just select that date and time, and create the blog in advance. You won't even have to be online when your blog is made available to viewers. Remember, too, that, while some people blog every day, others blog one to three times a week. The choice is yours. Whatever frequency you choose, however, do it regularly.

Read other blogs that post about topics that are relevant to your business and leave pertinent comments. Many blog writers have friends who read their blogs regularly, and also write blogs of their own. Leaving positive comments like this can help to generate valuable business connections without paying for advertising.

Consider holding a contest or competition from time to time to encourage reader participation and to attract new viewers. People may log in to view and participate in the contest, and then stay to view the rest of your website. Remember to post the names and photos of contest winners on your website, so people will travel to your website to admire their pictures and learn who won the contest. You may also want to try to enhance sales potentials by featuring special offers directly beside contest results. Then, visitors who stop by to read about the contest will see these prominently posted offers and then continue to browse for more great deals.

Another option is to offer bloggers free products to inspect and review. Design your layout so that you can post contests, discount offers, or freebies next to or below the review. Offer points to visitors who make the most relevant and informative comments about your blogs and reviews, and offer a freebie to the top contributors.

Use your blog to keep readers informed about the latest events in your business world. Introduce new products, offers, and services. Some visitors prefer reading brief blog entries to full feature articles, so keep blog posts concise, relevant, and entertaining.

Develop a blogging routine and stick to it, so readers know what to expect. You may not have many readers initially. Growing a good readership requires time and good content. Consider adding stories from real customers about how your business helped or affected them positively, but never use their real names without first obtaining their permission. Keep content personable, but avoid becoming too personal. Use a light conversational or humorously entertaining tone when writing.

Newsletters

Newsletters are usually easier to write and less time consuming than blogs. Publish them weekly or monthly by email. This will help to keep readers informed without overwhelming them. Don't overdo graphics and photos in a newsletter, because these will take longer to download.

Update readers about current events, special bargains, new articles or information, and include a brief statement from you, the owner. Feature new associates or business partnerships. Always publish the newsletter regularly and on time, or you may lose the trust of your readers – which means losing the trust of your customers or clients.

Summing it up:
Good social networking platforms include:
- Facebook
- Twitter
- LinkedIn.

Successful networking profile creation involves:
- Being personable without getting too personal
- An appropriate, professional, but relaxed photo
- The casually professional representation of your company.

Blogs and journals offer:
- A virtual journal where you can share daily events and special occasions
- Regular contact with readers (if you make timely and routine posts)
- An opportunity for readers to share their opinions about your products and services.

Chapter Ten: Evolve with the Times

"They say a year in the Internet business is like a dog year... equivalent to seven years in a regular person's life. In other words, it's evolving faster and faster."

- Vinton Cerf

Today, it's hard to imagine the world without the Internet. With an incredible amount of information and resources available at our fingertips, we no longer have to leave home to visit the library, attend school, talk to friends, or pay bills. We can buy and sell property without entering a real estate agency, or even visiting the property in question.

A quick review of the Internet's history emphasizes how rapidly the world has changed in the past three decades:

• In the 1980s, people began sending messages to one another through computers. Email became a feasible, though not yet popular, method of communication.

• In the early 1990s, three Internet commerce sites were introduced. Each of these has enjoyed incredible success and name recognition. Amazon.com, Craigslist.com, and eBay.com have all helped to make Internet business and marketing a feasible and attractive alternative for customers.

• Increasing speeds meant more graphics and text could be used on websites. This meant more advertising and more opportunities to attract visitors and potential buyers.

Today, e-commerce is incredibly popular. Business owners have many opportunities to expand their businesses and excel as a result of the almost limitless possibilities offered by the Internet.

Let's complete our discussion on web marketing with these last three topics:

• Your business is your business
• Keep content and copy current
• Stay three steps ahead.

Your Business is Your Business

Do you want to be seen as a guru in your field? Do you want readers and potential customers or clients to respect your opinions? Do you want viewers to follow your call to action? If the answer to any of these questions is "no", close your business now. You'll never succeed in the marketing world. If the answer to all of these questions, however, is "yes," you're ready for success.

To achieve success, you have to be able to offer visitors confident, knowledgeable, credible answers. Don't waste your time – or your visitors' time – by publishing anything else. Most visitors will search online to see if your answers are true. If they aren't, they'll tell you so – as they're walking out your virtual door to check out your competitors.

This may require taking some time to research your answers. It's always better, though, to take a few extra minutes and offer well-considered, intelligent answers, than to show your lack of knowledge by trying to fake your way through a situation. You may be able to fool a few people at least once, but most people will catch on after the first time. This is a very poor way to generate business!

Being successful also means staying informed as well as getting informed. If you were a computer guru in the 1990s, but didn't keep up with changes in microprocessor development or software applications, you're not much of an expert today. You don't have to make new discoveries every day to be respected in your field, but you do need to stay updated about the latest events, developments, and technologies in your field of expertise.

Become an expert about your competitors as well as about your field of knowledge. If you offer the best services in the country, but those services are twice as expensive as your competitors' services, you won't draw business. Learn about the prices, advertising methods, sales pitches, and the latest developments available from other professionals in your specialty area.

Be proactive rather than reactive. If you suspect a problem with a product or service that you offer, notify your clients and offer to work with them to correct the issue from the outset. Breaking the news yourself may be difficult, but your business will have a much better reputation if you share the information yourself than if the media tells your clients or customers.

Finally, know your audience. Understand the demographics of the people you serve. Research who your buyers are and what they expect. For example, don't deliver chatty, descriptive text content on a site targeted at meeting the needs of recreational hunters. Likewise, don't use college level terminology on a site dedicated to educating elementary children. Keep content appropriate to your clients and customers, so that your site meets their expectations – and their needs!

Always try to look, think, and see through the eyes of your clients or customers. Are you giving them exactly what they need? Does your site consistently offer information or products targeted to meet their demographics? Each time you post or update content, determine that the content will meet these objectives.

Keep Content Current

Stay current in your research, and keep your web content current as well. This doesn't necessarily mean adding new feature articles or updating content weekly. You can, however, add information about new developments regularly, and keep your website relevant to your audience. If you don't, people will stop visiting.

Search article directories, as well as industry publications and online journals, for news and information. Remember, by the time a journal article appears in print, it's already out of date. Don't rely on outdated information. Read the news online and stay informed about the latest issues on forums, trade sites, and competitors' sites. For example, if you specialize in herbal or alternative medicine, you will also want to stay updated about the latest concerns and issues with herbs, acupuncture, and other treatments. Stay informed as well about the FDA approval of the latest prescription medicines, and their side effects, so that you can maintain your expertise.

Keep social networking profiles updated too. If you listed goals on your site that you met or completed or revised six months ago, your profile is outdated. If you don't keep your profile updated with new details and information, regular clients will stop visiting. Additionally, new visitors will notice that you haven't updated your profile in months and think that you are no longer active. Then they will be much less likely to visit your business website.

If you blog, blog regularly. Never promise to give more information about a subject and then fail to deliver. Visitors will notice that you failed to deliver on that promise and wonder whether they can trust your business practices. Whether you blog once daily or once weekly, develop a routine and stick to it.

If you listed charitable organizations or community involvement on your profile, or note them on your website, keep content about these organizations current. If you post that you are still sponsoring a community Little League baseball team, but have pictures on your website that show Johnny posing as a catcher (when he is now the coach), your credibility will be seriously diminished. Posting updated content shows your involvement and your concern. Since your goal is to share your involvement and concern with visitors, meet that goal with current content.

Similarly, if you post content about affiliate sites, ensure that the information about those sites remains current. Keep readers updated on changes in business hours or locations. Remove broken links, and check links regularly to make sure they are working. If you post content about specials or discounts offered by these affiliates, update your website when those offers are no longer available.

When to Update

Staying ahead of your competition is essential to keeping your business healthy. You can achieve this, at least in part, by keeping your content updated. Try to report news or technological developments that are directly related to your business field as soon as possible, unless this news will have a negative effect on your business.

Most people are quick to pass on exciting breakthroughs, but fewer people pass on industry updates that may lead to exciting advances. Stories like these can serve as a bright spot to people desperately seeking hopeful news. Try to find positive and hopeful news to share whenever possible.

If new laws or historical events have affected your business, don't be afraid to share your opinions. Just keep the opinions professional, and remember not to bash competitors, lawmakers, or individuals on your website, social networking site, blog, or newsletter. Personal attacks often come back to haunt the attacker, so avoid this pitfall. Likewise, tread cautiously regarding any topics concerned with politics or religion - these topics can start intense arguments quickly.

Always post status updates or changes on your company website as soon as possible. If you just added a new partner, or if a trusted associate will be leaving the company, share this information to keep your clients and customers informed. Of course, it doesn't hurt to post personal information as well, like a marriage, milestone birthday, or new addition to the family.

If your company or organization plans to offer new products or services, start informing readers as soon as you're ready to meet the demand. Just don't advertise before you're ready. If you start advertising services you can't yet offer, or can offer only on a limited basis, you may lose new clients who expect you to deliver on your advertising immediately.

Product recalls do occur and you have a legal obligation to report them if you carry or use those products. If you don't carry or use those products, but they are relevant to your business, consider whether reporting them might be harmful to your business.

For example, if you own a daycare business, you may want to keep parents informed on recalls of infant strollers or safety seats. A travel agency, however, may not be so keen on reporting the latest recall of an airline's entire fleet of planes, because this would likely have a negative effect on airline travel for quite some time.

Always, confirm that what you are reporting is true. Take time to do the research. Otherwise, this will have a negative impact on your reputation. For example, most of us receive emails from time to time about urban legends or virus alerts. Some people take the time to verify the information before passing it on; others pass it on and have to be told by their friends that it isn't true. Don't put yourself in this potentially embarrassing situation; always verify information before sharing it as fact.

Conclusion

We've discussed a lot of information in this book. If some of the content was very new or unfamiliar to you, you may find it helpful to go back and re-read a chapter or two. Take time to fully digest the information, and then start using it to make your mark in the world of Internet commerce.

In each of the preceding chapters, we've shared key concepts and vital information that can be utilized to design and market a website for a business. Whether you choose to attempt this on your own, or entrust your business success to a professional web design and marketing team, you can use this information to make your business successful. Reap the financial rewards of your business success. Develop a business plan for monetary growth and stick to it. Soon, you'll see that the sky is the limit to your financial rewards!

Content is king. Keep that saying in mind. Stay alert, focused on your business, and always keep an eye out for new content. Post it in an appropriate location, and update it as needed. If you remember all of these things, you have the necessary tools to take your Internet business venture to new heights. Implement these concepts, follow the guidelines, and watch your business grow!

INDEX

A

about us page   17
acronyms   6, 8, 12
advertises   103-4, 124
advocacy sites   41, 67
agency   39, 46, 91, 125
airline   125
announcements   47, 49, 58-9
answers   39-40, 54, 56, 88, 120
applets   98
applications   31, 44-5, 98
area businesses   57
article directories   87-8, 92
attention   72, 98, 108
   reader's   72-3
   visitor's   28
attorneys   46, 48
audio   45

B

backlinks   86
basics   3, 25
Better Business Bureau   89
biographical   66
blog site   58, 112
bloggers post links   58
blogs   43, 60, 103, 112-15, 123-4
bonuses   73, 75
bored reader   27
browsers   97-9
browsing   26, 30
budget   91, 93
   daily   91
business   3-12, 16-17, 20, 25-6, 28-30, 33-4, 39-41, 46-8,
      53-4, 59-60, 87-9, 97-8, 103-6, 108-14, 119-21, 123-6
business card   107
business competitor   9
business connections   89, 110, 113
business contacts   109
   potential   110
business correspondence   25
business entity   11
business experiences   111
business field   124

129

D

internet   18-19, 27, 29, 31, 55, 67, 79, 82, 111, 119
internet business   117, 119
internet business venture   126
internet business world overnight   29
internet Explorer   97
interviews   29, 44-6, 49, 56-7, 72
invitations   47, 49, 58-9

J

java   98-9
javaScript   98-9
journals   67, 112, 115

K

keyword phrases   80, 82-3, 90-1
  page's   81
keywords   79-80, 82-3, 85, 90-1, 112
knowledge   106, 120-1

L

language   37, 39, 55, 70
layout   25, 28-33, 35, 83, 113
  website's   83
layout design   27, 65
lead-ins   42
legal services   69, 74
link building   80, 86-7, 92
linkbacks   58, 86
LinkedIn   104, 108-10, 115
links   18, 28, 42, 45, 57-8, 60, 67, 80, 84, 86-90, 105-9, 123
  broken   123
load   19, 53, 73
local business arena   89
local businesses   30, 58, 108
local community library resource page   89
location   10, 35, 72-5, 80, 110, 123, 126
logo   4, 16-18, 25, 29
lose business   7

M

market web design services   70
marketing   3, 53, 59, 65, 68, 103, 105, 119
marketing approach   4-5
marketing strategies   3-4

133

profile   105, 108, 110-12, 122-3
  premium business   109
promise   123
promotional   40-1, 66-7
property   19, 119
prospective visitors   6
publicity, free   88-9

Q

quality content   33, 36
  high   28
quality graphics, high   21
quality service   40
quality writers   34
questions, visitor's   39

R

rate, conversion   65, 71
readability   29, 33-4, 36, 55
readability level   33
reader participation   113
readers   28, 31-2, 35, 41-5, 48-9, 54, 59, 67, 70-3, 75, 87-8,
    90, 114-15, 120, 123
reader's eye   15, 32, 35
reader's interest   43, 70
reciprocal links   87
region   10
register   10-11, 73, 88-9, 92
registering   6, 9, 11-12, 85
registration   41, 68, 74, 112
registry   8, 11
remind readers   48
reputable businesses   60
reputation   44, 121, 125
resources   55, 98, 119
review websites, manually   86
right Graphics   18

S

sales sites   40, 66-7
Sam   43-4
Sam's website   44
scripts   86, 99
search engine marketing (SEM)   77, 79, 84, 86, 90, 92
search engine optimization *see* SEO

LaVergne, TN USA
24 February 2011
217810LV00002B/212/P